A Popular Guide to the
Preserved Steam Railways of Britain

Colin Garratt

GW00600601

BLANDFORD PRESS
Poole   Dorset

Blandford Press Ltd,
Link House, West Street,
Poole, Dorset BH15 1LL

First published 1979
Copyright © 1979 Blandford Press Ltd

ISBN 0 7137 0978 2

British Library Cataloguing in Publication Data

Garratt, Colin Dennis
   A popular guide to the preserved steam railways
   of Britain. – (Blandford colour series).
   1. Railroads – Great Britain – History
   2. Locomotives – Great Britain – History
   I. Title
   385'.0941   HE3018

ISBN 0–7137–0978–2

Set in 10/11½ pt. Ehrhardt and
printed and bound in Great Britain by
Butler & Tanner Ltd, Frome and London

Colour printed by Sackville Press
(Billericay) Ltd

Contents

A. *Passenger-carrying railways with a defined route mileage*

B. *Live steam museums with rides provided around yards or grounds*

C. *Museums and static collections*

Acknowledgements

The author and publishers wish to thank the following for supplying the photographs for this book:

Paul Barber (plate 1); Geoffrey King (plate 2, pages 56, 64, 65, 100, 111, 122, 127, 128); M. Crowe (plate 3); David Williams (plates 4, 5, 11, 20, 24, 25, 26, 28); Fred Butler (plates 6, 9, 13, 15, 19, 31, 34); John Marsh (plates 7, 17, 35, 39, 40); Roger Crombleholme (plate 8); Graham Scott-Lowe (plate 10, pages 16, 30); Caroline King (plate 12); Mike Woods (plate 14, pages 36, 38, 45, 90); Geoffrey Monks (plates 16, 18, 24, 37, page 92); Shane's Castle Railway (plate 21); Bicton Woodland Railway (plate 22); Geoffrey Silcock (plates 23, 29, 30, pages 14, 18); A. Thompson (plate 32); Judy Warner (plate 33); Donald Wilson (plate 36, page 34); Norman Gurley (plate 38); Maurice Burns (pages 15, 141); Frank Dumbleton (pages 19, 51, 52); Rex Coffin (pages 28, 84); John Gardner (pages 41, 50, 62, 78, 87, 95, 119, 134, 142); Brian Stephenson (page 43); Nene Valley Railway (page 69); John Titlow (page 70); National Railway Museum (page 138); Peter Robinson (page 143); Peter Westwater (page 150); Bill Robertson (page 153); Charles Friel (pages 158, 159); Valerie Burns (endpaper).

The endpaper photograph shows ex-LMS 'Black 5' 4767 'George Stephenson' making an impressive start out of Levisham with the Grosmount-bound North Yorkshireman in 1977.

Author's Note

This small book is designed to act as an introduction to the sixty-five principal places at which steam locomotives can be enjoyed in Britain. It is hoped that the ensuing pages will stimulate further interest in the wonderful achievements made by railway preservationists over the last thirty years.

The information given was correct at the time of writing, but the steam preservation scene is, by its very nature, one of permanent change. Engines move from one establishment to another, while many of the railways themselves are in a constant state of development. However, where major changes are expected—such as extensions in the route mileage—I have anticipated them in the text.

Furthermore, the opening and operating times mentioned are likely to change somewhat from year to year, and a few of the small establishments will not necessarily run steam locomotives every day. I have therefore included the address and telephone number of the railways so that intending visitors may check in advance. Groups are always welcome, and preserved railways are ideal centres for parties of schoolchildren on study courses. (Please enclose a s.a.e. if writing.)

The layout of the book is self-explanatory, and the lines are arranged within their geographical divisions so that those nearest each other on the map are also close together in the text. (One superb way of seeing a range of lines is to obtain the weeekly season ticket offered by the Great Little Trains of Wales.) Although primarily concerned with preserved railways run by volunteers, I have included a few exceptions—such as the Snowdon Mountain Railway—for obvious reasons. I have also featured several significant Museum collections.

Visitors can assume that excellent car parking and toilet facilities exist at the vast majority of centres. Refreshments are also freely available, and many trains carry a buffet car. In addition every centre has sales stands for souvenirs and items of local interest, along with a comprehensive selection of railway books.

A tribute to the preservationists themselves. It has taken years of toil and dedicated enthusiasm to ensure that the steam railway does not fade into oblivion. However, volunteers are still urgently needed by many lines if their survival is to be assured. If you are prepared to offer your help I urge you to get in touch with the railway of your choice. You will receive a warm welcome, and will be contributing towards one of the most exciting developments in Britain today.

I am indebted to the photographers who have contributed so many fine pictures to this book, and also to Roger Crombleholme for his help in collating the illustrations and in making so many valuable suggestions towards the book as a whole. Finally, I thank my wife Stephanie for typing the manuscript.

Colin Garratt

The Railway Preservation Movement

During the 1950s no one imagined the extent to which railway preservation in Britain would aspire. For in those years steam locomotives were an unquestioned part of the nation's transportation system, and although their eventual demise had been decreed under the Railway Modernization Plan of 1955, a new decade was to dawn before the last example was built. Equally, no one anticipated how rapid the demise of steam would be once it started: by 1968 the steam locomotive—with all its inbuilt simplicity and longevity—was extinct on Britain's main-line railways.

When Britain's railways were nationalized in 1948, the new administration inherited over 20,000 steam locomotives embracing hundreds of different classes. Many were legacies from the old private companies, almost all of whom designed their own engines; others were the products of the big four—LMS, LNER, GWR and SR—formed at the 1923 grouping. In an attempt to rationalize the multitude of different types, British Railways increased the diversity by introducing their own range of standard classes in 1951. In addition, thousands more steam locomotives of an entirely different order could be seen in industrial service.

The interest and excitement provided by British railways throughout the 1950s attracted millions of people to the linesides. When the end of steam finally came, the nation's railway enthusiasts rallied to fight a vigorous rearguard action, joining forces to save as many locomotive types as possible as class after class of Britain's locomotive heritage was ruthlessly cast aside. The limited number of engines earmarked to become static exhibits in the National Collection was poor recompense for all that was being lost.

The preservation movement began in 1950, when the run-down 2 ft 3 in. gauge Talyllyn Railway in Central Wales was taken over by enthusiasts determined to renovate and operate the entire system. Before this no railway had been preserved anywhere in the world, and only a very limited selection of engines and rolling stock represented the developments of the previous one-and-a-half cen-

13

turies. Cynics claimed the whole idea was preposterous: enthusiasts could never run a railway. But the Talyllyn pioneers did succeed, and they were not alone. Four years later the abandoned 1 ft 11½ in. gauge Festiniog Railway was acquired on a similar basis, and in 1955, after immense legal, financial and practical problems had been overcome, the trains ran again.

As the movement gained momentum, attention was inevitably focussed on the standard gauge, and in 1958 a scheme was started to reopen a section of the LBSCR's 'Bluebell Line' in Sussex. Again the cynics spoke out: enthusiasts might be able to run trains on narrow-gauge lines, but standard-gauge railways with full-sized engines were out of the question. But the preservationists triumphed; a scrap contractor was prevented from lifting the rails in 1959, and the Bluebell Railway Preservation Society began operating steam services in 1960. From then on, preservation schemes proliferated, and a new railway mania was born.

As the steam engine was phased out, Britain's railway network—

Southern 'S15' 30841 'Greene King' is seen here leaving Manningtree bound for Ely in 1976. Today the engine's endeavours continue undiminished on the Nene Valley Railway.

A member of the North Eastern Locomotive Preservation Group stands in the firebox of the LNER 'KI' 2005, beading over new tubes in the boiler.

once the finest in the world—was partially destroyed. The iniquitous 'Beeching Plan' shut down innumerable lines, and although this action was of dubious value in the national interest it provided a heaven-sent opportunity for preservationists; all over Britain closed lines became the subject of appeals. Imaginative fund raising combined with enormous loans raised the huge deposits which had to be paid to prevent BR from lifting the tracks of abandoned lines, and ensured the success of many schemes. Preserved engines and items of rolling stock began to gravitate to various centres throughout the country.

The total restoration of a derelict railway is a task of frightening magnitude. The outlay needed for track and land alone is enormous, but the costs and work involved in the restoration of stations and signal boxes, along with the provision of adequate workshops and covered accommodation for stock, must also be taken into account. Restoring a withdrawn locomotive to working order invariably costs thousands of pounds, especially when new parts have to be manufactured. In short, railway preservation is no task for groups of people who merely want to play with trains. Safety standards must be rigidly adhered to and a high standard of administrative competence proved before the Ministry of Transport will grant the necessary Light Railway Order for passenger services to commence.

Many railways operate as registered charities in order to benefit fully from money subscribed by deed of covenant. The companies are limited by guarantee, having no share capital—every penny earned being reinvested. Virtually all rely upon volunteer help from members of a supporting society. The complexities of the movement as a whole are ably co-ordinated by the Association of Railway Preservation Societies (ARPS), a non-profit-making body comprising a team of fully qualified advisers who assist with a wide range of technical, legal and administrative problems. The ARPS also provides a national publicity campaign and links the private pre-

Woodham's Scrapyard at Barry in South Wales. This reserve of condemned engines has given preservationists time to raise funds to purchase engines for restoration.

servation movement with such bodies as British Rail, the British Tourist Authority, Department of Education and Science and the Transport Trust. Almost all railway preservation societies in Britain are members of ARPS.

Much had been achieved in railway preservation by the time BR abandoned steam, but after years of feverish activity the preservationists' resources were inevitably strained, and as the last BR steam engines were despatched to breakers' yards it seemed as if the period of preserving main-line engines was irretrievably closed. Abandoned branch lines—with or without track—might still be secured, but there would be no more engines.

Miraculously, there was one exception: Woodham's Scrapyard at Barry in South Wales. Here engines had been allowed to accumulate during the 1960s, and in 1968—when virtually every other yard in the country had cut up their steam locomotives—Woodham retained some two hundred examples. Over the next ten years some seventy engines—representing many historically significant classes—were purchased from this graveyard for eventual restoration on preserved lines. Indeed some of the rusted hulks dragged out of the Barry scrapyard are among Britain's most celebrated steam engines today.

Unfortunately, many distinguished locomotive types were extinct before the preservation era gathered strength, for example the passenger classes of the London & North Western and Great Central railways. However, most major classes of the post-grouping period are represented, some of them very prolifically, such as the fifteen LMS Stanier 'Black 5' 4–6–0s and the thirteen GWR '5700' Class 0–6–0 Pannier Tanks. The most numerous pre-grouping class are the LBSCR's 'Terrier' 0–6–0Ts with twelve examples in existence, several of them over a century old.

Hundreds of industrial engines—the products of some forty different builders—are to be found on preserved lines throughout the country. The best known type is the Hunslet Austerity 0–6–0 Saddle Tank of which more examples have been preserved than of any other steam class in the world. Originally built for Army service during the European Invasion in 1943, over fifty Austerities have been saved, and numbers continue to increase as further engines are acquired from various industrial establishments—notably the National Coal Board.

A brace of BR Standard 2MT 2–6–0s lie deep in Barry graveyard. First introduced in 1953 all sixty-five locomotives of this class had been condemned by 1967.

In addition to the home preservation effort, many locomotives of various gauges are coming to Britain from overseas. These have included British built engines exported at various times over the last eighty years, along with others of purely foreign design. A few preserved British engines have also gone overseas including a GWR 'Castle' 4–6–0 and a LNER 'A4' Pacific.

During the 1970s an entirely new dimension in railway preservation began when a full sized working replica of Stephenson's *Locomotion No I* of 1825 was built for the 150-year celebrations of the Stockton & Darlington Railway held at Shildon in 1975. Three years later working replicas of engines which took part in the Rainhill Trials of 1829 were built in readiness for the Liverpool & Manchester Railway 150-year celebrations in 1980. Other moves in creating new types are the planned rebuilding of a GWR 'Hall' 4–6–0 into a 'Saint' class engine by the Great Western Society, Didcot, and these may be the beginnings of a new phase of development.

Part of the overhauling process for GW '28XX' Class No. 3822 at Didcot. Protective clothing is essential when removing asbestos lagging from locomotive boilers.

The preservation scene constitutes a miracle. Who would have believed ten years ago that British Rail—after their vitriolic rejection of steam traction—would again be advertising 'Full Steam Ahead—For all the Family'! During the summer of 1978 BR commenced operating steam services on regular days between York, Leeds and Harrogate; also between Carnforth and Sellafield, using such glorious engines as 'Flying Scotsman', 'Sir Nigel Gresley', 'Green Arrow' and 'Evening Star'. The following year steam services were reintroduced between York and Scarborough—a turntable having been installed specially at Scarborough for a total cost of £50,000!

Steam locomotives might be regarded as Britain's greatest technological gift to mankind; let us hope that they will continue to be enjoyed by future generations.

Area 1. South-West

DART VALLEY RAILWAY

HQ and Location
Buckfastleigh Station, Buckfastleigh, Devon. Buckfastleigh is situated on the A38 Exeter–Plymouth road. Torquay 16 miles. Exeter 22 miles.

Track Route
Buckfastleigh–Totnes (7 miles). Gauge: Standard.

Times of Opening
Daily throughout peak summer months.

Further Information from
Dart Valley Railway Co., Buckfastleigh Station, Devon. Tel: Buckfastleigh 2338.

Using Great Western engines and coaches, the Dart Valley Railway line follows the River Dart through seven delightful miles of Devon countryside, from Buckfastleigh to Totnes. Trains include the 'Devon Belle' observation coach once used on this famous express which ran from Waterloo to North Devon.

The Dart Valley line was originally a broad-gauge branch from Totnes up to Ashburton on the edge of Dartmoor. It was opened in 1872, and conversion to standard gauge was not effected until twenty years later. British Railways closed the line in September 1962, but during the same month news appeared that a group of businessmen planned to reopen the line as a private enterprise. The Dart Valley suffered a particular tragedy in its early years when the line was severed by improvements to the A38 Exeter–Plymouth trunk road. Everything possible was done to avert this catastrophe, but the upper reaches of the line had to be abandoned to allow

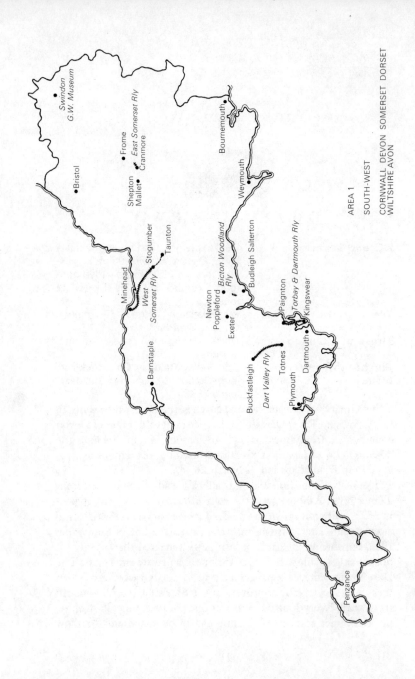

Swindon
G.W. Museum

Frome
East Somerset Rly
Cranmore

Bournemouth

Bristol

Shepton
Mallet

Weymouth

Stogumber
Taunton

Bicton Woodland
Rly

Budleigh Salterton

Minehead

West
Somerset Rly

Newton
Poppleford
Exeter

Paignton
Torbay & Dartmouth Rly
Kingswear

Barnstaple

Buckfastleigh

Dart Valley Rly
Totnes
Plymouth

Dartmouth

Penzance

AREA 1

SOUTH-WEST

CORNWALL DEVON SOMERSET DORSET
WILTSHIRE AVON

part of the track bed to be incorporated into the new highway. Thus the restored Ashburton Station with its towering roof was lost to the railway, and trains now terminate at Buckfastleigh. Ashburton's lovely station still exists—ironically—as a garage and filling station.

Despite this disaster the Dart Valley Railway has prospered to become one of Britain's most celebrated and best loved lines, thanks to the dedicated help of a keen supporters' society—the Dart Valley Railway Association—which, although not legally tied to the company, undertakes much valuable voluntary work.

Motive power is predominantly Great Western with 14XX class 0–4–2Ts and several classes of Pannier Tanks including No. 1638 'Dartington' built in 1951 as a 16XX—a GW design which did not appear until after nationalization. One can also see GW Prairie 2–6–2T No. 4555 'Gladiator', one of a large class of secondary line engines which saw extensive use in the west country. On the heavier side is No. 4920 'Dumbleton Hall' (built Swindon 1929) and No. 5239, a 2–8–0T named 'Thunderer' built in 1924 as a 52XX class heavy mineral engine to a design introduced by Churchward in 1910.

Passengers can join the Dart Valley Railway at Buckfastleigh or Staverton Bridge, but at present no access is provided to the railway from the town at Totnes. A connecting line with British Rail has been retained and this enables the company to interchange engines and rolling stock with their other line, the Torbay and Dartmouth Railway.

TORBAY AND DARTMOUTH RAILWAY

HQ and Location   Paignton Queens Park Station, Devon. Access from Paignton BR Station, Paignton Town Centre.

Track Route   Paignton–Kingswear (7 miles). Gauge: Standard.

Times of Opening   A steam service operates daily from April until the beginning of October.

Torbay & Dartmouth Railway, Paignton Queens Park Station, Paignton, Devon. Tel: Paignton 555872.

The Dart Valley Railway Company made an imaginative expansion when they took over the Paignton to Kingswear line upon its closure by British Rail in 1972. This lovely line runs through spectacular scenery and offers panoramic views of Torbay and the Dart Estuary. Included in the seven-mile journey are high viaducts, a tunnel five hundred yards long and gradients as sharp as 1-in-60. Trains take half an hour in each direction, with stops at Goodrington Sands and Churston. Kingswear platform is situated at the water's edge, and passengers can take the ferry over the estuary to Dartmouth.

Pride of the line is No. 7827 'Lydham Manor', built after nationalization in 1950 and upon withdrawal in 1965 sold to Woodham Bros of Barry for scrap. She was purchased by the Dart Valley Company and was moved during June 1970 to Buckfastleigh where she was fully restored to working order and then transferred to the Torbay line. Another engine often seen at Torbay is ex-GWR Prairie 2-6-2T No. 4588 'Warrior' built in 1927. She was also rescued from Barry and, following her major overhaul at Swindon Works in 1971, has worked in Devon ever since. The Torbay line shares its coaches and engines with the Dart Valley, and members of the Dart Valley Railway Association assist in running the line.

When their green and copper coloured 'Manor' heads a train of cream and chocolate coaches past the gorse-strewn embankments and red cliffs of Torbay she makes one of the finest sights in British steam preservation. Go and sample the magic for yourself.

BICTON WOODLAND RAILWAY

HQ and Location
Bicton Gardens, Budleigh Salterton, Devon. Situated on the west

	side of the A376 between Budleigh Salterton and Newton Poppleford. Exeter 12 miles. Torbay 33 miles.
Track Route	A main line through the gardens plus a lakeside branch (1⅓ miles). Gauge: 1 ft 6 in.
Times of Opening	The grounds are normally open in the afternoons from Easter until the end of October.
Further Information from	The Agent, Rolle Estate Office, East Budleigh, Budleigh Salterton, Devon.

These celebrated gardens date back to 1735 and were designed by Andre Le Notre, gardener to Louis XIV at Versailles. The decision to open them to the public was not made until 1961, after Bicton House had been sold. A substitute attraction was needed—and what better than a narrow-gauge steam railway?

The initial survey revealed a necessity for tight curves and steep gradients, thus demanding a large engine with short wheelbase. A derelict 1 ft 6 in. gauge 0–4–0T named 'Woolwich' was discovered in a scrapyard at Brackley, Northamptonshire. After examination the engine was jacked up clear of the ground for a steam test. Despite rust and peeling paint the engine 'marked time' perfectly amid clouds of steam and a smell of hot oil. Two days later, she arrived at Bicton to help construct the railway.

'Woolwich' was built by Avonside of Bristol in 1916 for the narrow-gauge lines of the Royal Arsenal Woolwich. She is an oil-burner, and to raise steam wood is burnt in the firebox until the boiler pressure reaches 20 lb per sq. in.: sufficient to activate the oil-feed cock. Thereafter pressures rises swiftly to 160 lb per sq in., the working maximum.

Starting from Bicton Gardens station the line passes the 'Countryside Museum', containing steam engines and farm vehicles, before skirting the lake over which Bicton House can be seen. Continuing over an embankment the line enters a beautiful Pinetum—first planted in 1840. Having reached Pine Junction the railway loops around the Lower Pinetum, which includes the Wilson Collection of trees brought to this country by E. M. Wilson, the celebrated botanist and plant collector.

WEST SOMERSET RAILWAY

HQ and Location	Minehead Station, Somerset. Situated on the A39 Bridgwater–Barnstaple road. Bridgwater 25 miles. Taunton 21 miles.
Track Route	Diesel Railcars: Minehead–Stogumber (13 miles). Steam Trains: Minehead–Blue Anchor ($3\frac{1}{2}$ miles). Gauge: Standard.
Times of Opening	Diesel railcars running throughout the year; steam services during holiday times.
Further Information from	West Somerset Railway, The Railway Station, Minehead, Somerset. Tel: Minehead (0643) 4996.

In 1971 British Rail closed the twenty-five mile line from Taunton to Minehead despite much local opposition. The West Somerset Railway Company was subsequently formed to reopen the line in its entirety as a private enterprise, and the long battle which ensued was finally won when the Somerset County Council purchased the line from British Rail and leased it to the company. As a result of much dedicated toil, diesel railcars are already running regularly between Minehead and Stogumber, and steam services are added between Minehead and Blue Anchor during the holiday season.

The original West Somerset Railway was opened in 1862 and—in common with the East Somerset—was laid to the 7 ft broad gauge. In 1882 the line was converted to standard gauge—the changeover being completed between the last train one Saturday and the first train the following Monday morning.

The line leaves Minehead and passes below the Norman castle at Dunster before running alongside the sea at Blue Anchor. Next comes Washford, to be the centre for the steam locomotives of the Somerset and Dorset Museum Trust. A further attraction here is the superbly preserved 13th century Cleeve Abbey. Having passed through the ancient seaport at Watchet, the train heads inland to Williton, the last surviving example of a Bristol and Exeter broad-gauge station. This historic site is scheduled to become the base of the Diesel and Electric Group and Britain's first exclusively diesel railway preservation centre. The final station is Stogumber (the line's terminus at time of writing).

The West Somerset Railway achieved fame with Independent Television's six-part railway adventure 'The Flockton Flyer', which featured its ex-GWR 0-6-0 Pannier Tank No. 6412 in the title role. Other motive power on the line includes two huge 0-6-0STs named 'Vulcan' and 'Victor', built in 1950 and 1951 respectively by Bagnall of Stafford for the Steel Company of Wales. Later ousted by diesels they ended their pre-preservation days at Austin Motors' Longbridge Works in 1973.

Three ex-GWR 2-6-2Ts rescued from the Barry scrapyard are also to be seen along with the notable Fowler 2-8-0 No. 58308, one of a class first introduced in 1911 for working over the gradients of the Somerset and Dorset Railway. This engine—also saved from Barry—is owned by the Somerset and Dorset Railway Museum Trust who have further enlivened the West Somerset with their range of industrial 0-4-0/0-6-0 Saddle Tanks and with a Bagnall 0-4-0 'Fireless' which worked at the Huntley and Palmer biscuit factory at Reading until 1970.

Progress on the railway is proceeding apace, and the company now have their sights firmly set upon reaching Taunton. Extensions to the steam services will also be made.

EAST SOMERSET RAILWAY

HQ and Location   Cranmore Station, Cranmore, Somerset. Situated on the A361 Frome—Shepton Mallet road. Shepton Mallet 3 miles. Frome 9 miles. Longleat 12 miles. Bristol 19 miles.

Two engines of Lord Fisher's Locomotive Group on the East Somerset Railway. On the left is ex-LMS 'Jinty' 47493 with Andrew Barclay 0–4–0 ST 'Lord Fisher'.

Track Route	Yard area only at present. Gauge: Standard.
Times of Opening	Daily throughout the year with locomotives in steam on Sundays during the summer.
Further Information from	East Somerset Railway, Cranmore Station, Cranmore, Somerset. Tel: Cranmore 417.

This marvellous railway owes its existence to artist David Shepherd, well-known for his wildlife paintings and a noted railway artist. His success enabled him to purchase two fine examples of British Railways' standard steam classes introduced in the 1950s.

By far the best known is the '9F' 2–10–0 No. 92203, built at Swindon in 1959 and purchased upon withdrawal from Birkenhead shed in 1967 after a ridiculously short working life of eight years.

Subsequently named 'Black Prince', this 2–10–0 is famous for working BR railtours. The other standard type is Class 4 4–6–0 No. 75029, built at Swindon in 1954 and also withdrawn in 1967. This engine, now painted in BR standard green, is named 'The Green Knight'.

Having purchased the engines, there was then the problem of finding a suitable home for them, and after an eighteen-month search Cranmore was discovered. Originally this station was part of the broad-gauge East Somerset Railway which ran from Witham to Shepton Mallet. The gauge was changed to standard on incorporation into the GWR in 1874. The line was closed to passenger traffic in 1963.

In addition to the renovation of Cranmore Station and the conversion of the signal box interior into an art gallery a brand new Victorian engine shed has been built. Classified 82H, this 4,000 sq. ft building is 130 ft long, and has two roads complete with inspection pits and extensive overhaul facilities. During November 1973 David Shepherd's two BR standards steamed overnight from Eastleigh to Cranmore hauling trains of preserved rolling stock, and the centre was formally opened by HRH The Prince of the Netherlands in June 1975.

A worthy addition to the East Somerset is ex-Southern Railway Schools Class 4–4–0 'Stowe', jointly owned with Lord Montague. Cranmore's motive power roster has been further enhanced by No. 9 'Cannock Wood', a former London Brighton and South Coast Railway Class 'E1' 0–6–0T built in 1877 as one of a class of 73 engines built by Stroudley between 1874 and 1884. Several other engines are to be seen at Cranmore, and it is hoped that steam trains will eventually operate as far as Shepton Mallet and possibly beyond.

GREAT WESTERN MUSEUM SWINDON

HQ and Location   Emlyn Square, Swindon, Wiltshire. Ten minutes walk from Swindon main line station.

Times of Opening	10.00 am–5.00 pm Monday to Saturday; Sunday 2.00 pm–5.00 pm.
Further Information from	The Curator, Great Western Museum, Farringdon Road, Swindon, Wilts. Tel. Swindon (0793) 26161.

Swindon is synonymous with railways: it was the first of Britain's 'railway towns', and home of the Great Western for over a century. It is fitting that this noble tradition should be commemorated in Swindon by a beautiful museum.

The main hall is called the Churchward Gallery and contains five resplendent locomotives. First comes a full-sized replica of 'North Star', built in 1837 and forerunner of the crack 'Firefly' and 'Iron Duke' classes which raced westwards from Paddington over Brunel's magnificent 7 ft gauge main line. Next is a Dean 'Goods': 260 of these classically proportioned 0–6–0s were built between 1883 and 1899. They were trusty 'maids of all work' for

Great Western Railway 0–6–0 Pannier Tank No. 6412 crosses Broadsands Viaduct with the 16.30 Paignton–Kingswear.

the entire GW system; many were sent abroad during both world wars and some were destroyed by enemy action.

Alongside stands 'City of Truro', the handsome outside-framed 4–4–0 which made history on 9 May 1904 by hauling the Plymouth Ocean Mails special from Exeter to Bristol at an average speed of over 70 mph, and exceeded 100 mph during the descent of Wellington Bank. Nearby is No. 4003 'Lode Star', an example of Churchward's four-cylinder 4–6–0 express passenger engines. When introduced the Stars were years ahead of their time and they formed the basis for the later Castles and Kings which so ably served the Great Western for the remainder of its existence. Fifth in succession is No. 9400, a GW Pannier Tank designed by F. W. Hawksworth. This engine represents the final design of Pannier and the last GW class to appear before nationalization.

The museum is also notable for its excellent collection of paintings, photographs, headboards, nameplates and other railway memorabilia, including some superb models. Pride of place is given to the silver-plated model of a Gooch 'Firefly' class.

Area 2. South-East

MID-HANTS RAILWAY (WATERCRESS LINE)

HQ and Location Alresford Station, Alresford, Hampshire. Alresford is situated on the A31, halfway between Winchester and Alton. Winchester 9 miles.

Track Route Alresford–Ropley (3 miles). Gauge: Standard.

Times of Opening Saturday afternoons; Sundays and Bank Holiday Mondays from mid-March to end of October.

Further Information from Winchester and Alton Railway Ltd., Alresford Station, Alresford, Hants.

The original Mid-Hants Railway, opened in 1865, ran through seventeen miles of delightful countryside between Winchester and Alton. Both ends of the line connected with the London and South Western Railway. The Mid-Hants was popularly known as the 'Watercress Line' since Alresford was a principal source of this commodity and, during the season, up to nine tons a day would be carried. Absorbed into the LSW in 1884, the line passed into Southern Railway ownership at the 1923 grouping, and to British Railways upon nationalization in 1948.

British Railways attempted to close this useful cross-country route in 1968, but fierce opposition caused the line to be retained for a further five years. Efforts towards preservation began prior to closure when the Winchester and Alton Railway Company determined to operate the line privately with a daily diesel service supported by steam tourist trains. The sum of £100,000 subsequently raised was insufficient to save the whole line, and contracts were exchanged in June 1976 with British Rail for purchase of the land and track between Alresford and Ropley, along with the land and buildings over the remaining seven miles to Alton. The section

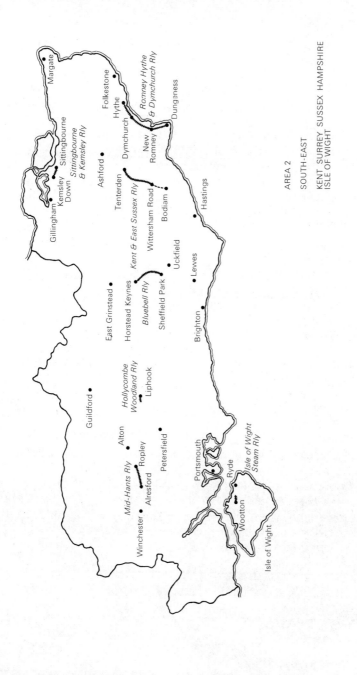

AREA 2

SOUTH-EAST

KENT SURREY SUSSEX HAMPSHIRE
ISLE OF WIGHT

Margate

Folkestone

Hythe

*Romney Hythe
& Dymchurch Rly*

Dungeness

Sittingbourne

Kemsley
Down *Sittingbourne
& Kemsley Rly*

Dymchurch

New
Romney

Ashford

Gillingham

Kemsley

Tenterden

Kent & East Sussex Rly

Wittersham Road

Bodiam

Hastings

Uckfield

Lewes

East Grinstead

Horstead Keynes

Bluebell Rly

Sheffield Park

Brighton

Guildford

*Hollycombe
Woodland Rly*

Liphook

Alton

Petersfield

Mid-Hants Rly

Ropley

Alresford

Winchester

Portsmouth

Ryde

*Isle of Wight
Steam Rly*

Wootton

Isle of Wight

between Winchester Junction and Alresford was abandoned. The Alresford to Ropley section was reopened with great enthusiasm on 30 April 1977, and the company intend to relay the Ropley–Alton section as funds permit.

Today a splendid selection of Southern locomotives can be seen on the railway. The oldest is ex-LSWR Urie No. 30506 built at Eastleigh in 1920 and now owned by the Urie S15 Preservation Group. The post-grouping period is represented by two Moguls: 'U' Class No. 31806—originally built as a River 2–6–4T—and 'N' Class No. 31874 'Aznar Line'—the engine which hauled the opening train.

Two West Country Pacifics represent latter-day Southern practice: No. 34016 'Bodmin' in rebuilt form and No. 34105 'Swanage' in her original Bulleid air-smoothed casing. Many locomotives are undergoing restoration to working order at Ropley, where the company intend to build their engine sheds and workshop. A number of industrial engines can also be seen, and ex-Army Austerity 0–6–0ST No. 196 'Errol Lonsdale' was very active during the

Ex-Southern Railway 'N' Class Mogul 31874, now named 'Aznar Line', is seen here durir the Mid-Hants Railway celebrations in April 1977.

first season; this engine came from the nearby Longmoor Military Railway.

Volunteer staff for the Winchester and Alton Railway Company are recruited from the two-thousand-strong membership of the Mid-Hants Railway Preservation Society.

ISLE OF WIGHT STEAM RAILWAY

HQ and Location	Haven Street Station, Nr Ryde, Isle of Wight. Service 3 of Southern Vectis buses operates from Ryde Esplanade or Newport and stops outside Haven Street Station.
Track Route	Haven Street–Wootton (1¾ miles). Gauge: Standard.
Times of Opening	Sundays from May to September; Thursday afternoons during July and August, and Bank Holidays between Easter and September.
Further Information from	Isle of Wight Steam Railway, Haven Street Station, Nr Ryde, Isle of Wight. Tel: Wootton Bridge 882204.

In 1966 a group of London-based enthusiasts formed the Wight Locomotive Society; their aim was to secure for posterity an ex-London and South Western Railway '02' Class 0–4–4T. The 02s had worked the island's trains for many years, and the society succeeded in rescuing W24 'Calbourne' from the breaker's torch along with a number of vintage coaches. The next stage was to restore the engine to full working splendour. After negotiations with the Isle of Wight County Council the Haven Street–Wootton section of the old Ryde–Newport line was leased to the society. Having now found a base, the society formed the Isle of Wight Railway Company in readiness for operating services. The original station

35

Hawthorn Leslie 0–4–0ST 'Invincible', built for shunting duties at Woolwich Arsenal during World War I, enters Haven Street Station with a train from Wootton.

at Wootton had been closed in 1953 and the site demolished by an earth slip, so the company built a new terminal station with run-round facilities.

In June 1971 the company's second engine arrived in the form of 'Invincible'—an 0–4–0ST built by Hawthorn Leslie in 1915 for use during World War I at the Woolwich Arsenal. She had ended her pre-preservation days with the Royal Aircraft Establishment at Farnborough, hauling coal and stores from British Rail to the RAE. The next engine acquired was 'Ajax', an 0–6–0T built by Andrew Barclay in 1918. After a long and chequered career—which included a spell with the Anglo Persian Oil Company in Persia—'Ajax' ended her days with British Steel at Harlaxton.

Ex-London Brighton and South Coast Railway 'Terrier' Class 0–6–0T reached the island during 1973. She was built at Brighton Works in 1878 as No. 40 'Brighton' and represented her company at the Great Paris Exhibition that year where she won a Gold

Medal. In 1902 the LBSCR sold her to the Isle of Wight Central Railway, and in 1930—under Southern Railway ownership—she was renamed 'Newport'. Eventually ousted by the more powerful 02s, 'Newport' returned to the mainland in 1947 and passed into British Railways stock. She spent her final days as No. 32640 on the Havant–Hayling Island line until withdrawal from service in 1963.

In 1975 the Isle of Wight Railway Company celebrated the centenary of the Ryde and Newport Railway, and this set a precedent for the 1976 Summer Steam Show, which included steam lorries and fire engines and attracted 5,000 visitors.

Leaving Haven Street, the line climbs steeply at 1-in-66; embankments alternate with cuttings, while the copses and peaceful meadows suggest a timeless rural landscape.

HOLLYCOMBE WOODLAND RAILWAY

HQ and Location	Hollycombe Woodland Gardens, Liphook, Hants. Liphook is situated on the A3 road between Guildford and Petersfield. Nearest BR station: Liphook (access to railway).
Track Route	Through the grounds of Hollycombe House. Gauge: 2 ft ($\frac{1}{2}$ mile); Standard (300 yards).
Times of Opening	Saturdays, Sundays and Bank Holidays between Easter and October from 2.00 pm.
Further Information from	Hollycombe House, Liphook, Hants. GU30 7LP.

The gardens of Hollycombe were laid out at the turn of the century by J. C. Hawkshaw, who was responsible for planting over a million trees—including many rare species—on the 4,000-acre estate. The narrow-gauge railway runs to the sand quarry which once supplied the estate with building materials, and from here the visitor can enjoy spectacular views of the South Downs. The engines, track and much rolling stock came from the famous Dinorwic Slate Quarry near Bangor. Two engines are to be seen: 'Caledonia', an 0–4–0 Well Tank built by Andrew Barclay of Kilmarnock in 1931 and 'Jerry M', an 1895-built 0–4–0ST from Hunslet of Leeds.

A fine contrast is provided on the standard-gauge tramway. Here, passengers can take a ride behind 'Sir Vincent', an 0–4–0TG built in 1917 by Aveling and Porter of Rochester (the famous makers of steamrollers). This remarkable engine—complete with flywheel—is a cross between a ploughing engine and a railway locomotive and is further characterized by the Kent horse 'Invicta' on the smoke box door.

Among other treasures at Hollycombe are a steam-driven roundabout, razzle-dazzle, cakewalk and swings, and 'Greenwich Gem', a horse-drawn fire engine of 1903. The collection also contains 'Princess Mary'—possibly the finest showman's engine in existence today.

Mr W. H. McAlpine's 1906-built Aveling Porter 0–4–0TG 'Sirapite' tundles along with an old GW 20-ton 'Toad' brakevan at Fawley Hill near Henley-on-Thames.

The magnificent spectacle of steam ploughing may also be seen powered by 'Empress of India', built by McLaren in 1881 and possibly the oldest traction engine in regular use today. Meanwhile, at the railheads of the quarry railway and tramway, a Grafton Crane grabs stone from a bank and demonstrates the transfer from narrow to standard-gauge vehicles.

BLUEBELL RAILWAY

HQ and Location	Sheffield Park Station, Nr Uckfield, East Sussex. Sheffield Park is situated halfway along the A275 road between East Grinstead and Lewes. London 40 miles. Nearest BR stations: Haywards Heath; Uckfield.
Track Route	Sheffield Park–Horsted Keynes (5 miles). Gauge: Standard.
Times of Opening	Daily from June to September; Wednesdays, Saturdays, Sundays during May and October; Saturdays, Sundays during March, April and November; Sundays during January, February and December; Boxing and New Year's Day.
Further Information from	Bluebell Railway Ltd, Sheffield Park Station, Nr Uckfield, East Sussex. Tel: Newick (082–572) 2370.

In March 1959 three students called a public meeting at Haywards Heath in an attempt to save the Bluebell Line—a part of the ex-London Brighton and South Coast Railway's route from Lewes to East Grinstead. Initially their scheme sounded incredible—not least to British Railways—but, within two years, the Bluebell Railway Company had been formed, and a section of the line reopened from Sheffield Park. This was Britain's pioneer standard-gauge scheme, and its success came during a time of much cynicism towards railway preservation. In 1962 services were extended from Sheffield Park to Horsted Keynes, the present terminus, and by 1968 the line had been paid for outright. Plans are now well under way to extend the railway to East Grinstead, which would give the line a connection with British Rail.

Sheffield Park Station vividly recreates the original LBSCR characteristics: the paintwork is purple-brown and stone, oil lamps and LBSCR signals are in use, and many fine relics of the Victorian/Edwardian era can be seen—including enamel advertisements. Horsted Keynes, in contrast, has been restored to evoke the atmosphere of a Southern Railway station, with green paintwork, electric lights and Southern signals. But the station itself forms a lasting monument to the 'railway age', with the sheer size and magnificence of the buildings.

A running shed and locomotive works have been built at Sheffield Park, and many engines are available for visitors to inspect.

Three engines are ex-LBSCR: the lovely 0–6–2T 'Birch Grove' of Billington's 'E4' Class and two Stroudley 'Terrier' 0–6–0Ts—one of which is the 107-year-old 'Fenchurch'. Five engines represent the South Eastern and Chatham Railway: three 'P' Class 0–6–0Ts, the priceless Wainwright 'H' Class 0–4–4T No. 263 and the ever popular 'C' Class No. 592, a typically British 0–6–0 goods engine of 1902. The London and South Western Railway is represented by two engines: No. 488—one of the elegant Adams Radial Tanks built for suburban traffic from Waterloo in 1885—and the diminutive 'B4' 0–4–0T 'Corrall Queen'.

From the Southern Railway comes Maunsell 'U' Class 1618 rescued from the Barry scrapyard and now owned by the Maunsell Locomotive Society. The visitor will also see West Country Pacific 21C123 'Blackmore Vale', resplendent in her original air-smoothed casing and complete with chain-driven valve gear. This engine belongs to the Bulleid Society. Another Bulleid engine is 'QI' Class 33001: the final design of inside cylinder 0–6–0 goods engines and the most powerful. She belongs to the National Collection but is on loan to the Bulleid Society for restoration, with the Bluebell as custodians.

One final engine must be mentioned: the unique outside-framed

An air-smoothed Bulleid Pacific at the head of the Atlantic Coast Express. The Bluebell Railway recreates past splendour with the help of 21C123 'Blackmore Vale'.

ex-Great Western 4–4–0 'Earl of Berkeley'—last survivor of the 'Dukedogs' built during the 1930s from parts of older Duke and Bulldog engines. Most of the Bluebell Railway's locomotives and coaches are already fully restored to their original liveries.

KENT AND EAST SUSSEX RAILWAY

HQ and Location   Tenterden Town Station, Tenterden, Kent. Tenterden is situated on the A28 Ashford–Hastings road. Nearest BR stations: Headcorn or

41

	Ashford; then by bus to Tenterden.
Track Route	Tenterden Town–Wittersham Road (4 miles). Gauge: Standard.
Times of Opening	Saturdays and Sundays from end of March to end of October; Wednesdays during June and July; daily throughout August; Sundays during November and December; Christmas Holidays and New Year's Day.
Further Information from	Tenterden Railway Co. Ltd, Tenterden Town Station, Tenterden, Kent. Tel: Tenterden (05806) 2943.

The Kent and East Sussex Railway was the first standard gauge line to be built under the Light Railway Act 1896; it was engineered and operated by Colonel Holman F. Stephens—the uncrowned king of British light railways. Opened in stages between 1900 and 1905, the KESR ran from Robertsbridge—on the London–Hastings main line—along the Rother Valley to Tenterden and thence to Headcorn, connecting with the Tonbridge–Ashford line.

Upon closure in 1961 a preservation society was formed to restore the section from Tenterden to Robertsbridge. This scheme encountered innumerable difficulties and legal battles, but in February 1974, thirteen years later, the KESR reopened its first section with passenger trains running from Tenterden to Morghew Crossing just beyond Rolvenden. The terminus has since been extended to Wittersham Road and upon returning the trains face a heavy slog over the 1-in-50 Tenterden Bank.

The Company intends to reopen and operate the ten-mile section from Tenterden to Bodiam, and renovation work has been speeded up by a £95,000 grant from the Manpower Services Commission to employ forty young people under the job creation scheme. The Tenterden Railway Company is a registered charity.

Over twenty steam engines are on the railway including two ex-London Brighton and South Coast Railway 'Terrier' 0–6–0Ts named 'Bodiam' and 'Sutton', built in 1872 and 1876 respectively. 'Bodiam' worked on the original Rother Valley line 75 years ago! Another gem is the ex-South Eastern and Chatham Railway Class 'P' 0–6–0T 'Pride of Sussex', built in 1909.

More modern 0–6–0Ts are provided by 'Wainwright' and 'Maunsell', a pair of World War II US Army Transportation Corps engines which ended their days shunting in Southampton Docks. One of the finest engines on the line is ex-Norwegian State Railway No. 19, a willowy Mogul which fits the light railway atmosphere of the KESR to perfection.

A splendid range of industrial engines are also to be seen in various stages of restoration.

The 1976 steam up and locomotive cavalcade attracted 5,000 people in two days. Eight engines were in steam, and a special ceremony was held to celebrate the hundredth birthday of 'Terrier' Class 'Sutton'.

On Summer Saturday evenings you can travel on the Wealden Pullman and enjoy a four-course dinner complete with wine. The meals are served in pre-war splendour in coaches with inlaid walnut panelling and individual armchair seats.

A stirring scene on the KESR with ex-Norwegian Mogul No. 19 at the head of a passenger train.

ROMNEY HYTHE AND DYMCHURCH RAILWAY

HQ and Location New Romney Station, Kent. Hythe and New Romney are on the A259 road from Folkestone to Hastings. Nearest BR station: Folkestone Central, then by bus routes 94 or 95 direct to the Hythe RHDR station.

Track Route Hythe–Dungeness (13¾ miles). Gauge: 1 ft 3 in.

Times of Opening Daily from beginning of April to end of September; Saturdays and Sundays during October and November; Sundays during March.

Further Information from The Manager, Romney Hythe & Dymchurch Railway, New Romney, Kent. Tel: New Romney (06793) 2353.

Known popularly as the 'World's Smallest Public Railway', the RH&D is guaranteed to thrill even the most casual visitor. The line is operated by eleven steam locomotives covering five different classes, and on a busy day over twenty steam trains can be seen at New Romney.

Engine numbers 1, 2, 3, 7 and 8 are modelled on the ex-LNER A3 Pacific, of which 'Flying Scotsman' is the only survivor, while numbers 5 and 6 were built for freight workings and are 4–8–2 variants of the same type; all were built during the 1920s. Number 4 is a contractor's engine which actually helped to construct the railway fifty years ago. Numbers 9 and 10 were built slightly more recently—in 1931—and are based on light Pacifics of the Canadian National Railways. However, the most recent engine is No. 11, built by Krupp in 1937 and based on a design of Bavarian Pacific.

Built by Capt. J. E. P. Howey, the Romney Hythe and Dymchurch Railway was opened between 1927 and 1929, and was intended to provide a freight and passenger service to a remote part

of the Kent coast. It was conceived as a miniature working repro-
duction of a fully equipped and up-to-date main line railway; it
has become a living museum of the great steam age. The trains
carry two hundred passengers and run at 25 mph.

A loop at Dungeness enables special trains to run non-stop from
Hythe and back; this 28-mile journey is by far the longest steam-
hauled run on any preserved line in Britain today. The railway owns
over seventy passenger coaches, the majority fully enclosed and
weatherproofed, but some with open sides for the summer months.

During World War II the RH&D was taken over by the Army,
and an armoured train was built as part of this mobile defence.
In 1945 the railway was handed back in an extremely run-down
condition and, after rejuvenative toil, it was officially reopened
in 1947.

Captain Howey died in 1963, and his ashes were buried in New
Romney station yard. Today the railway is controlled by a con-
sortium headed by Bill McAlpine and Brian Hollingsworth.

*The Romney Hythe & Dymchurch Railway's 1 ft 3 in. gauge Davey Paxman 4–8–2 No. 6
'Samson' prepares to leave New Romney with a passenger train.*

SITTINGBOURNE AND KEMSLEY LIGHT RAILWAY

HQ and Location Sittingbourne and Kemsley Station, Sittingbourne, Kent. Sittingbourne is reached from Exit 5 of the M2 motorway. Nearest BR station: Sittingbourne (5 minutes' walk). No public access to Kemsley Down.

Track Route Sittingbourne—Kemsley Down (2 miles). Gauge: 2 ft 6 in.

Times of Opening Saturdays and Sundays from end of March to early October; Tuesdays, Wednesdays and Thursdays during August; Christmas and Bank Holidays.

Further Information from Sittingbourne & Kemsley Light Railway, Kemsley Down Station, Sittingbourne, Kent. Tel: Sittingbourne 24899 (operating days only).

This railway was opened in 1906 by Edward Lloyd Ltd to transport paper from Milton Creek to Sittingbourne Mills. Later the line was extended out to Ridham on the Swale, where a new dock had been built to receive imported logs and paper pulp. In 1924 another mill was built at Kemsley, and so a thriving industrial railway system was formed with several miles of main line which remained in use twenty-four hours a day until after World War II.

In 1948 Lloyd were taken over by Bowater, but the railway continued, and by the mid-1950s thirteen steam locomotives were in operation. In 1965, however, it was decreed that a road system should replace the railway. Bowater were successfully approached by the Locomotive Club of Great Britain, under the auspices of the Association of Railway Preservation Societies, and leased them a two-mile section of line between Sittingbourne and Kemsley. The

Sittingbourne and Kemsley Light Railway Company was formed to operate and maintain the line on a non-profit-making basis.

The S&K inherited six locomotives from Bowater: three 0–4–2STs—including two of Edward Lloyd's original engines of 1905 named 'Premier' and 'Leader'—and three 0–6–2Ts. The railway also has a large 2–4–0 'Fireless' as a static exhibit. Engines not in use are displayed at Kemsley Down, where the society plans to create a leisure area and museum in addition to their engine sheds and workshops.

Set in fine industrial surroundings, the line begins with a quarter-mile viaduct spanning Milton Creek before heading away through marshy fields. A journey provides views of the fine parish church at Milton, and the Swale—which separates the Isle of Sheppey from the mainland—is visible in the distance.

Passengers are carried in the former workmen's coaches, and in addition the S&K has about fifty freight wagons. Some of these are in regular use and it is intended to restore a representative selection to their original condition. Normal service is enhanced by special events including traction engines, fairground organs and miniature railways. On 'Enthusiasts' Day' freight trains are run and an emphasis is placed upon lineside photography.

Area 3. Home Counties

THE SCIENCE MUSEUM

HQ and Location	The Science Museum, South Kensington, London SW7. The Museum is situated on Exhibition Road, South Kensington. Nearest tube station: South Kensington on the Piccadilly, District and Circle Lines.
Gauge	Standard; 5 ft.
Times of Opening	Weekdays and Sunday afternoons.
Further Information from	The Director, The Science Museum, South Kensington, London SW7 2DD. Tel: (01) 589 6371.

Internationally famous for its diverse range of industrial and technological exhibits, the Science Museum contains some noteworthy locomotives and is now London's leading railway museum.

One of the most interesting exhibits is the renowned 'Puffing Billy', built at Wylam Colliery, Northumberland, in 1813 by William Hedley. This 12-ton archetype hauled 50-ton coal trains at 5 mph; it remained in service until 1862 and passed to the Science Museum the following year.

Far more celebrated is Stephenson's 0–2–2 'Rocket', built in 1829 for the Liverpool and Manchester Railway. Popularly regarded as the first steam locomotive ever built, 'Rocket' had some twenty-nine predecessors, though it did embody several characteristics which later became standard in steam locomotive design. 'Rocket' was the winner of the famous 'Rainhill Trials' staged in 1829. Another competitor at the trials, 0–4–0 'Sanspareil', is also in the Science Museum.

AREA 3

HOME COUNTIES

OXFORDSHIRE BERKSHIRE
HERTFORDSHIRE BUCKINGHAMSHIRE
BEDFORDSHIRE LONDON

At the other end of the evolutionary scale is Great Western Railway No. 4073 'Caerphilly Castle' built in the autumn of 1923 as the first of the highly distinguished 'Castle' class.

GREAT WESTERN SOCIETY DIDCOT

HQ and Location Didcot Loco. Shed, Didcot, Oxfordshire. Didcot is situated ten miles south of Oxford and is easily reached from the A34 Oxford–Newbury road. Access through Didcot BR station.

Track Route Trips around the centre in the Great Western steam train. Gauge: Standard.

Times of Opening Bank Holidays and first and last Sundays of each month from Easter to October. Special steaming for schools in July. Hours: 11.00 am to 5.00 pm.

7808 'Cookham Manor' pilots 6998 'Burton Agnes Hall' at Didcot—two examples of the brilliant restoration work done by the Great Western Society.

killed work at Didcot as the tender of 6998 'Burton Agnes Hall' is restored to its former glory.

Further Information from

The Secretary, Great Western Society Ltd, Didcot; Oxfordshire, OX11 7NJ.

The Great Western Society was formed in 1961 to preserve some aspects of the GWR in full working order, and today a fabulous collection of locomotives and rolling stock—the largest devoted to any particular railway in the world—is housed in the old engine sheds at Didcot.

The depot, built by the GWR to a standard design in 1932, provides an authentic setting for the society's exhibits. It was taken over by the society in 1969 when it was closed by British Rail. The engine shed has four 200 ft roads and a heavy repair shop. The coaling stage is built up on an embankment, and supply wagons are shunted up to a central store from which the coal is fed into small skips in readiness for manual tipping into the engines below. A

Rescued from Barry, Great Western 'Castle' Class 5051 'Earl Bathurst' undergoes major res-toration to working order at Didcot.

75,000-gallon water tank forms the coaling stage roof. Unfortunately, the turntable had been taken out during the 1960s, but the society managed to replace it with a 70 ft example from Southampton Docks. The site now covers sixteen acres and is almost exclusively Great Western in content. It is affectionately known as 'Little Swindon'. There are over twenty engines, and some fifty coaches and wagons.

Didcot has become famous for its restoration work with such engines as 5900 'Hinderton Hall', 6998 'Burton Agnes Hall' and 7808 'Cookham Manor'. The society's train of fully restored GW coaches includes some 'Ocean Saloons' of the 1930s: 'Queen Mary', 'Prince of Wales' and 'Princess Elizabeth'.

In 1974 the society made history when 7808/6998 double-headed the vintage train on a railtour over British Rail metals—an event which won them the Association of Railway Preservation Societies' first annual award. Since then the train has made frequent railtours on BR, and in 1975 'Cookham Manor' took five coaches to Shildon to represent the GWR at the Stockton and Darlington 'Rail 150' exhibitions. All the excitement is not on BR, however, as Didcot has a demonstration line of its own.

Ten of Didcot's engines have been retrieved from Woodham's scrapyard at Barry, and a recent achievement was the restoration to main-line condition of 'Castle' Class 5051 'Earl Bathurst'. Other GW classes represented are 14XX 0–4–2T, 28XX 2–8–0, 4500 2–6–2T, 51XX/61XX 2–6–2T, 53XX 2–6–0, 56XX 0–6–2T, 72XX 2–8–2T, and, of course, the ubiquitous Pannier Tanks. The oldest engine at Didcot is 'Shannon', an 0–4–0WT built in 1857.

A milestone will be achieved when the GW Society convert 4942 'Maindy Hall' into a 'Saint' Class 29XX. The Saints, introduced in 1902 as a standard two-cylinder 4–6–0 design, were superb engines and provided the immediate forerunner to the 'Hall' Class; they were rendered extinct in 1953. This rebuilding creates an exciting precedent.

QUAINTON RAILWAY SOCIETY

HQ and Location
Quainton Road Station, Quainton, Aylesbury, Bucks. Take the A41 Banbury–Bicester–Aylesbury road; turn off for Quainton at Waddesdon. Aylesbury 6 miles. Nearest BR station: Aylesbury. (On Bank Holiday Mondays the 'Quaintonian' charter diesel train runs direct to Quainton from the station.)

Gauge
Standard.

Times of Opening
Engines in steam over Easter, Spring and Summer Bank Holidays and last Sunday in month from Easter to October. Centre open every Sunday from Easter to October. Hours: 10.00 am–6.00 pm.

Further Information from

Hon. Publicity Officer, Quainton Railway Society, 4 Kenton Avenue, Harrow, Middlesex, HA1 2BN. Tel: (01) 422 9964.

The Bank Holiday scene at Quainton Road is one of great animation. A busy steam-hauled passenger service around the centre is augmented by rides in wagons and on locomotive footplates. In contrast with the steam activities, the chartered diesel train 'Quaintonian' plies its way back and forth from Aylesbury BR Station.

It is strange to think that Quainton, set amid the peaceful Buckinghamshire countryside, was once a station on the London Metropolitan Railway. When the Manchester Sheffield and Lincolnshire Railway was extended southwards to become the Great Central it joined the Metropolitan line one mile north of Quainton. It was finally closed by BR in 1966 and stood derelict for three years, until the first engine arrived in the preservation era.

The society's origin goes back to 1962, when the London Railway Preservation Society was formed. The following year this group saved ex-Metropolitan Railway 0-4-4T No. L44 from the scrapyard and, after a desperate fund raising exercise, one of the lovely ex-LSWR Beattie 2-4-0 Well Tanks was added to their collection: No. 30585 built in 1874. Rolling stock and additional engines followed and Quainton down yard was secured to house them in 1969. In 1978 the ARPS guide listed 34 steam locomotives for Quainton—the largest stock in Britain. (The organization became known as the Quainton Railway Society in 1971.) A very large range of industrial engines can be seen along with ex-GWR Pannier Tanks, an Aveling Porter and several vertical-boilered Sentinels.

Several other societies and individuals keep their engines or stock at Quainton, notably the 6024 Preservation Group, who were responsible for rescuing ex-GWR 4-6-0 'King Edward I' from the Barry scrapyard. Another group is the Ivatt Locomotive Trust with a brace of '1200' Class 2-6-2Ts and a '6400' Class 2-6-0, and the Great Central Railway Coach Group has some magnificent rolling stock here including a Manchester Sheffield and Lincolnshire Railway six-wheeler. Further interest is added by the model railway from the Vale of Aylesbury Model Engineering Society.

If you cannot get to Quainton on one of its famous steaming days

54

a visit is worthwhile on Sunday during the season. (Some special mid-week steamings are arranged for school parties.)

LEIGHTON BUZZARD NARROW GAUGE RAILWAY

HQ and Location — Pages Park Station, Billington Road, Leighton Buzzard, Bedfordshire. Pages Park Station is situated on the east side of the A4146 road on the Hemel Hempstead side of Leighton Buzzard, half a mile from the town centre.

Track Route — Pages Park—Stonehenge Works (3 miles). Gauge: 2 ft.

Times of Opening — Bank Holidays and Sundays from mid-March to late September. Special party trips on certain Saturdays.

Further Information from — Leighton Buzzard Narrow Gauge Railway Society, Billington Road, Leighton Buzzard, Bedfordshire, LU7 8TN. Tel: Leighton Buzzard 3888.

The silica sand industry at Leighton Buzzard is a century old, and extensive quarries have been developed on the north-eastern side of the town. Initially, the sand was conveyed by horse and cart to the canal or railhead, but in 1919 a light railway was built to connect with the LNWR line from Leighton Buzzard to Dunstable.

Apart from its early period, the line was worked by small internal combustion engines, and for many years up to 3,000 tons of sand were carried each week. After World War II the rail traffic dwindled, and ceased completely in 1969 when the sidings at Leighton Buzzard were closed. Internal sand trains—operated by Joseph Arnold & Sons Ltd—still run over the northern section between Double Arches and Stonehenge. The southern section of

Tomorrow's enthusiast learns the classes, beginning with the Leighton Buzzard Railway's 2 ft gauge Orenstein & Koppel 0–4–0 Well Tank 'P. C. Allen'. A scene at Pages Park.

the line is now worked by the Leighton Buzzard Narrow Gauge Society, and seven splendidly varied steam engines have been collected.

Pride of the line is 'Chaloner', an 0–4–0 engine built by de Winton of Caenarvon in 1877. She is the last working example of some fifty similar engines built between 1875 and 1897 for the North Wales slate quarries. Her boiler is upright with a long thin chimney on top; the two cylinders are also set vertically. Some know her as the 'Coffee Pot', others as the 'Galloping Tea Urn', but whatever one's sentiments, she is an engine well worth seeing in action.

More conventional is the Kerr Stuart 'Wren' Class 0–4–0ST named 'Pixie'. This lovely engine was built in 1922 as part of an order for twenty-seven Wrens for a sewer contract at Barkingside in Essex. Then there is 'the Doll', an 0–6–0T built by Andrew Barclay in 1919 for an Oxfordshire ironstone pit.

'Rishra', an 0–4–0T from Bagleys of Burton-on-Trent in 1921, has an interesting story. Exported to India in 1922, she spent many years hauling coal. Her present owner is Mr M. Satow, formerly chairman of ICI in Calcutta, who discovered her derelict and rusty. Rescued and restored, she was shipped to England in two crates.

The remaining two engines at Leighton Buzzard are both Orenstein and Koppel Well Tanks: 'Elf', an 0–6–0 built in 1936, and 'P. C. Allen, an 0–4–0 of 1912. 'Elf' was supplied to the Cameroon Development Corporation and worked at the Tiko Rubber Mill. 'P. C. Allen' is believed to have worked her whole life in Northern Spain until brought back to England in 1963.

The Leighton Buzzard Railway is an excellent example of local industrial archaeology. The society is registered as a charity and is also incorporated as an Industrial and Provident Society. It is run and maintained entirely by volunteers.

WHIPSNADE AND UMFOLOZI LIGHT RAILWAY

HQ and Location	Whipsnade Zoo, Nr Dunstable, Bedfordshire. Whipsnade Zoo is on the south side of the B4540 road, $2\frac{1}{2}$ miles south of Dunstable.
Track Route	A circular line through the animal paddocks (3 miles). Gauge: 2 ft 6 in.
Times of Opening	Daily from the 1 April until end of October.
Further Information from	Pleasure Rail Ltd, 6 Chapman Crescent, Harrow, Middlesex. Tel: (01) 204 2681.

For many years Whipsnade Zoo has been a major attraction and in 1970 it was enhanced further by a narrow-gauge steam-worked railway. The railway provides an ideal means of seeing some of the larger animals at close hand; gradients, bridges and a tunnel are encountered during one journey, and the line is complete with signals operated from an ex-standard-gauge box. The railway's strange name is taken from the light railway on the Umfolozi Game Reserve in Natal from which many of Whipsnade's White Rhinos came.

All four steam engines came from the Bowater paper mills at Sittingbourne. 'Excelsior' is an 0–4–2ST from Kerr Stuart; 'Chevallier', 'Conqueror' and 'Superior' are all 0–6–2Ts from Manning Wardle, Bagnall and Kerr Stuart respectively. Ten thirty-seater passenger coaches are in use and these were rebuilt from Bowater bogie pulp wagons in 1970; they are fitted with longitudinal seats for easy viewing.

Also in the care of the railway is a 3 ft 6 in. gauge Class 7 4–8–0, originally exported from Glasgow to South Africa in 1896. She ended her days there as a station pilot at Johannesburg and was then sold to Zambia in 1971 to work on the Zambesi Sawmills Railway. This engine was given to artist David Shepherd by the Zambian Government and was returned to Britain. Eventually this exhibit will be transferred to the East Somerset Railway at Cranmore.

The Whipsnade and Umfolozi Railway is operated by Pleasure Rail Ltd, a commercial organization working in conjunction with the Zoological Society. (The line is not run by volunteer enthusiasts.)

KNEBWORTH WEST PARK AND WINTER GREEN RAILWAY

HQ and Location   Knebworth House, Nr. Stevenage, Hertfordshire. Knebworth House is situated 3 miles south of Stevenage. Direct access to Stevenage from the A1. Nearest BR station: Stevenage.

58

Track Route	Through the grounds of Knebworth House ($1\frac{1}{4}$ miles). Gauge: 1 ft $11\frac{1}{2}$ in.
Times of Opening	Daily from Easter to end of September. Steam engines operate at weekends and Bank Holidays plus one weekday during school holidays.
Further Information from	Pleasure Rail Ltd, 6 Chapman Crescent, Harrow, Middlesex. Tel: (01) 204 2681.

This comparatively little-known system made headlines in 1976 when a remarkable two-day narrow-gauge steam rally took place with nine 1 ft $11\frac{1}{2}$ in. gauge engines in steam. Over 6,000 visitors attended. The railway has much to offer under normal operating conditions, too, with five delightful locomotives of different types and backgrounds.

A classic British industrial design is represented at Knebworth by two Hunslet 0–4–0STs from Welsh slate quarries: 'Lilla' from Penrhyn and 'Lady Joan' from Dinorwic. Representing a different facet of British industry is Peckett 0–6–0ST 'Triassic' from Rugby Portland Cement at Southam.

Two engines hail from Reynolds Bros Sugar Estates in Natal, South Africa: a Bagnall 4–4–0T named 'Isibutu' and Avonside 0–4–0T 'Sezela'. These engines returned to Britain on a Union Castle liner and docked at Southampton in 1972. Finally, there is 'Sao Domingos', an Orenstein and Koppel 0–6–0WT from a Portuguese coal mine at Pedorido on the Banks of the River Douro.

Area 4. Eastern Counties

STOUR VALLEY RAILWAY

HQ and Location	Chappel and Wakes Colne Station, Essex. Halfway between Colchester and Halstead on the A604. Nearest BR station: Chappel & Wakes Colne (on the line from Marks Tey to Sudbury).
Gauge	Standard.
Times of Opening	Every weekend. Engines in steam on certain dates between March and October.
Further Information from	Stour Valley Railway Preservation Society, Chappel and Wakes Colne Station, Essex.

This society was formed to preserve the remaining eleven-and-a-half miles of the Stour Valley line between Marks Tey and Sudbury. At present the line is operated by a British Rail pay-train service and is grant-aided by local authorities. The line's future has been in doubt for some time and, pending its closure, the society have leased from British Rail the yards and station buildings at Chappel and Wakes Colne Station and converted them into a steam preservation centre. A fleet of locomotives and rolling stock has been assembled, and steam open days are held on certain days throughout the summer.

The society's intention is to purchase or lease the line from British Rail and operate a daily diesel passenger service augmented by steam-hauled trains at weekends. However, at time of writing it seems unlikely that BR will close the line in the near future. As

AREA 4

EASTERN COUNTIES

NORFOLK SUFFOLK ESSEX
CAMBRIDGESHIRE LINCOLNSHIRE
SOUTH HUMBERSIDE

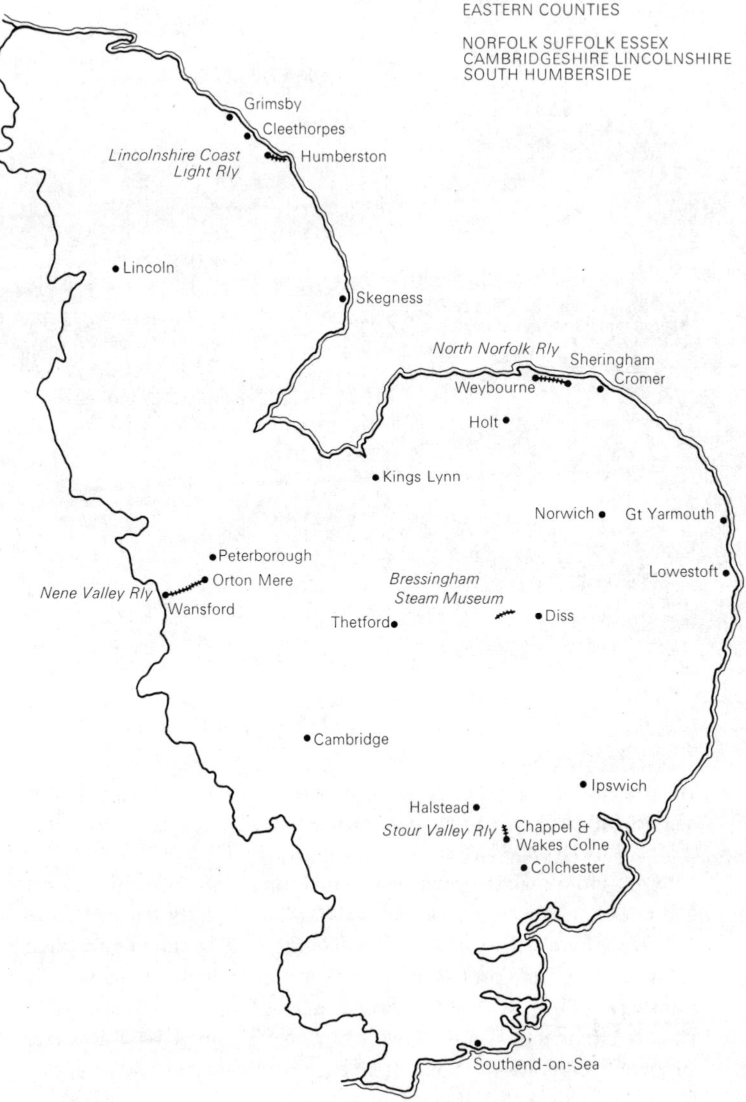

Grimsby
Cleethorpes
*Lincolnshire Coast
Light Rly* Humberston

• Lincoln

• Skegness

North Norfolk Rly Sheringham
Weybourne Cromer
Holt •

• Kings Lynn

Norwich • Gt Yarmouth

Lowestoft

• Peterborough *Bressingham
Steam Museum*
Nene Valley Rly Orton Mere
Wansford Thetford• • Diss

• Cambridge

• Ipswich

Halstead •
Stour Valley Rly Chappel &
Wakes Colne
• Colchester

Southend-on-Sea

Members of the Stour Valley Railway Society commemorate the end of steam at Harlaxton. The engine—Hunslet 0–6–0ST 'Gunby' is now at Chappel and Wakes Colne.

an alternative the society have considered restoring the Stour Valley line further north between Sudbury and Long Melford (subject to consent of the local authorities).

Meanwhile, some worthwhile exhibits can be enjoyed at Chappel, including ex-LNER 'N7' Class 0–6–2T No. 69621. The N7s were renowned for their work on the tightly timed suburban services from London Liverpool Street. Other engines include BR Standard 4MT 2–6–4T No. 80151, seen in contrast with a hefty Robert Stephenson and Hawthorn 0–6–0T, owned by Railway Vehicle Preservations. Some ten engines are present and an interesting collection of rolling stock.

BRESSINGHAM STEAM MUSEUM

HQ and Location
Bressingham Hall, Diss, Norfolk. $2\frac{1}{2}$ miles west of Diss on the A1066 road from Diss to Thetford.

Track Route
Footplate rides on standard-gauge engines. Narrow-gauge passenger trains running through the gardens. Gauge: Standard demonstration track (500 yds); 1 ft $11\frac{1}{2}$ in. (2 miles); 1 ft 3 in. ($2\frac{1}{2}$ miles); $9\frac{1}{2}$ in. (750 yds).

Times of Opening
Sunday afternoons from May to September; Thursday afternoons from last in May to mid-September; Wednesday afternoons during August; Spring and Summer Bank Holiday Mondays.

Further Information from
Alan Bloom, Bressingham Hall, Bressingham, Diss, Norfolk, IP22 2AB. Tel: Bressingham (037–998) 386.

The Bressingham story is a heartening one of the optimism and devotion of one man—Alan Bloom. At Bressingham a vast collection of herbaceous plants of amazing colour and diversity combine with one of the finest steam museums imaginable. The steam story began in 1961 when, having developed his celebrated gardens, Alan Bloom added several traction engines, which he and a small team of enthusiastic helpers restored to working order.

These were a great success with visitors and led to three narrow-gauge railways being installed throughout the grounds. A $9\frac{1}{2}$ in. gauge line was followed by a 1 ft $11\frac{1}{2}$ in. section using engines and stock from Penrhyn Slate Quarries in North Wales. Finally a 15 in. gauge line was laid using two handsome Pacifics built by Krupp of Essen in 1937. These passenger-carrying lines take visitors to all parts of the gardens.

British Railways Standard 'Britannia' 4–6–2 70013 'Oliver Cromwell' represents a marve of modern steam power in premature retirement at Bressingham.

It seemed a logical step for Alan Bloom to acquire some mainline engines. During winter 1967–8 a 12,500 sq. ft raft shed was erected, and British Rail's Curator of Historical Relics assigned the ex-London Tilbury and Southern Railway's 4–4–2T 'Thundersley' to Bressingham. Members of the Norfolk Railway Society worked upon her restoration.

Next came the stupendous news that 'Britannia' 4–6–2 'Oliver Cromwell' was to come to Bressingham immediately after working British Rail's last steam-hauled train from Liverpool to Carlisle on 11 August 1968. (She arrived at Bressingham on the 19th.) The next engine from BR was No. 2500, a Stanier three-cylinder 2–6–4T—the first of a type introduced in 1934 to replace 'Thundersley' and her sisters on the London Tilbury and Southern section of the LMS.

In 1970 arrangements were made for several Butlins steam locomotives to come to Bressingham on a permanent loan. These included ex-LMS No. 6100 'Royal Scot' and Stanier Pacific No. 6233 'Duchess of Sutherland'. Both have since been restored to working order and, along with 'Oliver Cromwell', are in constant demand for footplate rides.

Further engines arrived including 'Millfield', an 0–4–0 Crane Tank from Doxford's shipyard on the River Wear, and ex-Great Eastern 'J17' 0–6–0 No. 1217E—the last steam locomotive used by British Rail in East Anglia. One of Bressingham's most noted exhibits is 'William Francis', the last remaining standard-gauge Garratt in Britain.

Royal Scot' is one of Bressingham's many attractions. Here the celebrated ex-LMS three-cylinder 4–6–0 quietly simmers outside the museum.

Alan Bloom next turned his attention to classic continental designs, and his collection now includes a French '141R' Class 2–8–2—1,350 of which were sent to France from America to help build up the railways after the Nazi occupation. Another World War II type at Bressingham is the German '52' 2–10–0 bought from Norway. Over 6,000 52s were built; the second most numerous steam class in world history.

NORTH NORFOLK RAILWAY

HQ and Location	Sheringham Station, Sheringham, Norfolk. Adjoins the BR terminal station at Sheringham.
Track Route	Sheringham—Weybourne (3 miles). Gauge: Standard.
Times of Opening	Sundays during April and May and first half of October; Saturdays, Sundays, Wednesdays during June, July and September; Saturdays, Sundays, Wednesdays, Thursdays during August; Bank Holidays.
Further Information from	The Manager, North Norfolk Railway, Sheringham Station, Sheringham, Norfolk, NR26 8RA. Tel: Sheringham 822045.

Memories of the Midland and Great Northern Joint Railway evoke nostalgia among railway historians; its conglomeration of rambling rural lines, worked by beautifully designed engines in yellow-brown livery, was a highly distinctive aspect of the great railway age. Also known as the 'Muddle and Get Nowhere', the M&GN was an independent company run by a joint committee of the Midland Railway and Great Northern Railway. Its purpose was to give its parent companies access to the untapped areas of East Anglia, and the Great Eastern was its only competitor.

The M&GN survived the 1923 grouping—the LMS/LNER continuing to operate it jointly until 1936, when the LMS withdrew its interest. There followed a steady decline, and in 1959 much of the system was closed—the first major abandonment of a railway in Britain. Today East Anglia is dotted with the system's bridges, stations and earthworks; but no M&GN Railway locomotives exist today.

The North Norfolk Railway—conceived by the M&GN Railway Society—is committed to preserving a section of the original system, and its present service between Sheringham and Weybourne is over part of the old M&GN main line from Melton Constable to Cromer. However, the North Norfolk intend to extend from Weybourne towards the attractive market town of Holt.

A journey over the line is highly recommended. The line follows the coast by way of the cliff tops and provides lovely views; most of the journey to Weybourne is uphill with a maximum gradient of 1-in-80. Drivers on the A149 coast road gaze in wonder at such marvellous sights as a Peckett 0–6–0ST decked in M&GN yellow-gorse livery heading a train of ex-Great Northern articulated coaches. After crossing the road the line heads inland through rolling wooded farmland to Weybourne which is, at present, the terminus.

A real triumph was achieved when the society restored to full working order their ex-Great Eastern 'J15' 0–6–0 No. 564—the only survivor of a once prolific class which worked extensively throughout the Great Eastern network. Another sole survivor at Sheringham is ex-LNER 'B12' Class 4–6–0 No. 61572, built in 1912. Withdrawn from Norwich shed in 1961, she is the only inside cylinder 4–6–0 left in Britain, and although her restoration is long-term, she is a most imposing engine to behold.

Among a fine stud of industrials is Hunslet 0–6–0ST 'Ring Haw' from Nassington Ironstone Mine. This engine was once a companion to the Nene Valley Railway's 'Jacks Green'. One of the hardest worked engines is Kitson 0–6–0ST No. 45 'Colwyn', whose magnificent red livery is guaranteed to attract passengers. Altogether some ten steam locomotives can be seen on this particularly lovely railway.

NENE VALLEY RAILWAY

HQ and Location

Wansford Station, Old North Road, Stibbington, Wansford, Nr Peterborough, Northants. Wansford station is next to the A1 less than a mile from the A1/A47 intersection. Orton Mere Station is 4 miles from Peterborough City Centre.

Track Route

Wansford–Orton Mere (5 miles). Gauge: Standard.

Times of Opening

Sundays during April and May; Saturdays, Sundays, Thursdays during June and July; Saturdays, Sundays, Wednesdays, Thursdays during August; Saturdays, Sundays during September; Bank Holidays.

Further Information from

General Manager, Nene Valley Railway, P.O. Box 3, Peterborough, PE1 1UJ. Tel: 0733 68931 (Weekends: Tel: Stamford 782854).

British Rail's closure of the Nene Valley Line in 1972 coincided with the rapid expansion of Peterborough as a new town. The Peterborough Development Corporation planned to make part of the Nene Valley—through which the railway passed—a recreation area, and following the efforts begun by the Peterborough Railway Society it agreed to help reinstate a part of the line as a working museum and amenity through the leisure park. The Corporation bought the track and leased it to the society, who now operate the railway.

The line is part of the old Peterborough and Northampton Railway opened in 1845. This railway provided Peterborough with its first link to London, by connection from Northampton with the London and Birmingham. A cross-country route for over a century,

Oil-burning Swedish 2–6–4T No. 1928 with the inaugural through-freight working of fourteen BR wagons is seen here passing Orton Mere Station en route for Wansford.

the Nene Valley line linked Peterborough with Wellingborough, Northampton, Rugby and Birmingham, and in its final years it was noted for a wide variety of motive power.

From the outset the society embarked upon a policy of using British and Continental locomotives side by side, and adjustments were made to allow for the 'Berne Loading Gauge', including platform widening and demolition of a low road bridge. Three notable foreign engines have been bought by member Richard Hurlock: a Swedish 2–6–4T and 2–6–2T—oil and coal burners respectively—and an ex-Danish State Railway 0–6–0T built by Fricks of Aarhus in 1949. But the *pièce de résistance* is the French 'Nord' four-cylinder compound 4–6–0 complete in Nord brown livery. This engine was built in 1911 and is said to have run over two million miles. She is one of the few compounds working anywhere in the world today and is an engine worth crossing half of Britain to see in action. This masterpiece came to the Nene Valley by agreement with the Nord Locomotive Preservation Group.

Also at Wansford is the Southern Electric Group's unique set

The Nene Valley Railway's 'S15' 4–6–0 No. 841 'Greene King' bursts under Bettles Bridge, Castor, with a Christmas-time Santa Special.

of six ex-SR electric motor and trailer coaches. These make a fine contrast with the Norwegian coach once used on the suburban trains around Oslo, and the Nene Valley's cosmopolitan character reveals itself fully when the French compound works trains comprised of Southern Electric and Norwegian coaches travel through the East Anglian countryside.

Among well-known British engines is the BR Standard 5 4–6–0 73050 'City of Peterborough', bought from British Rail in 1968 by the Reverend Richard Paton, and the ex-Southern Railway 'S15' 4–6–0 'Greene King'. Another SR engine at Wansford is 34081 '92 Squadron' rescued from the Barry scrapyard by the Battle of Britain Locomotive Group; the restoration of this engine is but one of many exciting jobs to be tackled on the Nene Valley Railway.

Some celebrated industrial engines include Hudswell Clarke 0–6–0T 'Thomas'—of Reverend Audrey fame—and 'Jacks Green' from the nearby Nassington Ironstone Mine. This engine has been fully overhauled by apprentices at Peter Brotherhoods in Peterborough. Other items of interest include the 60 ft turntable from Peterborough East and the sixty-lever frame signal box at Wansford—possibly the largest preserved box on a British line and beautifully restored in original LNWR colours.

The Nene Valley Railway is also developing a freight service in conjunction with T. A. Hutchinson Haulage, whose premises are beside Wansford station.

LINCOLNSHIRE COAST LIGHT RAILWAY

HQ and Location   North Sea Lane Station, Humberston, Grimsby, Lincolnshire. Humberston North Sea Lane Station is situated on the east side of the A1031 two miles south of Cleethorpes. Buses from Grimsby Bull Ring and Cleethorpes Market Place.

Track Route	North Sea Lane—South Sea Lane (1 mile). Gauge: 2 ft.
Times of Opening	Daily from May to October. Steam at weekends.
Further Information from	The General Manager, Lincolnshire Coast Light Railway Ltd, North Sea Lane Station, Humberston, Nr Grimsby, Lincs.

In 1960 a group of Lincolnshire railway enthusiasts built this line to connect North Sea Lane bus terminus with Humberston beach and the nearby Fitties holiday camp. Two steam locomotives are used: a Peckett 0–6–0ST named 'Jurassic', which came from Rugby Portland Cement at Southam in Warwickshire, and 'Elin', a Hunslet 0–4–0ST of 1899 from Penrhyn Slate Quarries.

Some of the track and rolling stock came from the old 24-mile network of Nocton Potato Estates, but had previously done service in France during World War I. Several bogie coaches came from the Ashover and Sand Hutton Light Railways. This stock has been resuscitated and fitted with leather upholstered seats from Glasgow and Liverpool trams. Another interesting feature is the ex-standard-gauge signals, some from the Lancashire and Yorkshire Railway and others from the Great Northern (including an old somersault type).

Over 60,000 passenger journeys have been made here in one year, but quite apart from its functional use the railway serves as a permanent reminder of the many 2 ft gauge lines which once ran in Lincolnshire.

Area 5. Midlands

MIDLAND RAILWAY CENTRE

HQ and Location   Midland Railway Centre, Nr Ripley,
                       Derbyshire. The centre is situated
                       off the A61 road between Derby
                       and Chesterfield. Derby 11 miles.
                       Nearest BR station: Alfreton and
                       Mansfield Parkway; then by
                       National bus to Ripley, changing at
                       Alfreton bus station.
Gauge   Standard.
Times of Opening   Open weekends are held at regular
                       intervals.
**Further Information Midland Railway Trust Ltd, Ripley,
from**   Derbyshire.

The Midland was the third largest pre-grouping railway in Great
Britain and one of the best-managed systems in the world; its headquarters was at Derby. The Midland Railway Centre was conceived
by the former curator of Derby Museum, Mr A. L. Thorpe, whose
dream was to see a permanent memorial in the form of a working
museum dedicated to the Midland Railway, and its successor the
LMS.

In 1969 the Midland Railway Project Group was founded to
bring this dream to fruition, and every possible item relating to
the Midland Railway was avidly collected. The museum is situated
at Butterley on the closed connecting line which ran from Amber-
gate Junction on the old Midland route to Manchester across to
Pye Bridge Junction on the Erewash Valley line. It is intended that
the three-and-a-half-mile section between Hammersmith and Pye

73

Glossop

Dinting
Rly Centre

Chesterfield

Ripley

Stoke-on-Trent

Midland Rly Centre

Foxfield

Blythe Bridge

Foxfield Light Rly Derby

Nottingham

Loughborough

Shrewsbury

Shackerstone

Great Central Rly

*Chasewater
Light Rly*

*Shackerstone &
Bosworth Rly*

Wellington

Rothley

Market Bosworth

Leicester

Bridgnorth

Wolverhampton

Cadeby Light Rly

Severn Valley Rly

Hinckley

Bewdley

Birmingham

Birmingham Rly Museum

Northampton

Stratford upon Avon

Hereford

Bulmer Rly Centre

Gloucester

AREA 5

MIDLANDS

LEICESTERSHIRE DERBYSHIRE
NOTTINGHAMSHIRE NORTHANTS
WARWICKSHIRE WEST MIDLANDS
STAFFORDSHIRE WORCESTERSHIRE
HEREFORDSHIRE GLOUCESTERSHIRE
SHROPSHIRE

Bridge will become a working line for the exhibits. The centre will incorporate a locomotive shed, turntable, carriage shed and repair shops with a full range of maintenance facilities. A replica Midland station is being constructed along with period signals. This unique centre will eventually become an integral part of a wider-reaching leisure plan for the area. During 1973, the organization's name was changed to the Midland Railway Trust Ltd and, apart from being an educational charity, the trust receives support from Derby Corporation and Museum, Derbyshire County Council and Amber Valley District Council.

A fine collection of locomotives has been assembled, but pride of place must go to the graceful Johnson 4–2–2 'Spinner' No. 673—one of 95 engines built between 1887 and 1900. During 1978 this engine was returned to steam. Another Midland veteran is Kirtley 2–4–0 No. 158A, an outside framed passenger engine built at Derby in 1866.

Class '4F' 0–6–0 No. 44027 represents latter day Midland goods engines. She was built in 1924 and was one of 772 engines which were first introduced in 1911 by the Midland and were continued by the LMS after the grouping. Another Midland design perpetuated by the LMS was the 'Jinty' 0–6–0T. There are three of these at the Butterley museum including one restored in red livery.

The LMS's first Pacifics were the 'Princess Royals', and No. 6203 'Princess Margaret Rose'—now in LMS red livery—makes a stunning contrast with the Spinner. Withdrawn from Carlisle Kingmoor in 1962, 'Princess Margaret Rose' was saved by Sir Billy Butlin and exhibited at his Pwllheli Holiday Camp in North Wales. (The engine is on loan from Butlins.) Completing the larger exhibits is BR Standard 5 4–6–0 No. 73129 fitted with Caprotti valve gear.

Industrial engines from the 19th and 20th centuries are present and especially notable is an Andrew Barclay 0–4–0 Crane Tank built in 1925—one of several similar engines once used by Stanton and Staveley Works.

The centre's rolling stock is extremely interesting and includes a Midland Railway Pullman coach, a six-wheeled third coach of 1884 and a Royal Saloon dated 1910.

THE GREAT CENTRAL RAILWAY

HQ and Location	Loughborough Central Station, Loughborough, Leicestershire. Loughborough is situated on the A6 between Leicester and Derby and is also served by the M1 motorway. Leicester 12 miles. Central station is within 15 minutes' walk of BR Loughborough Midland station.
Track Route	Loughborough—Rothley (5 miles). Gauge: Standard.
Times of Opening	Trains run every Saturday and Sunday throughout the year and Wednesdays from end of May to early August.
Further Information from	Main Line Steam Trust Ltd, Great Central Road, Loughborough, Leics. Tel: Loughborough 216433. Registered office: 13 New Street, Leicester, LE1 5NP. Tel: Leicester 21443.

In 1969 a group of enthusiasts met in Leicester with the intention of preserving a working steam main line over which trains would run at express speeds. The line chosen was part of the old Great Central route southwards from Loughborough. Constructed as recently as 1899 the GC was the last main-line railway to be built in Britain and was fully capable of taking the largest locomotives. The GC's Chairman, Sir Edward Watkin, intended this railway to be part of a through-route to the continent via the proposed Channel tunnel. Accordingly the new line was constructed to continental loading gauge.

The Great Central evolved from the provincial Manchester Sheffield and Lincolnshire Railway, and the extension was made southwards from Annesley through Nottingham, Loughborough,

Leicester, Rugby and Brackley, after which a connection was made with the Metropolitan just north of Quainton Road and the GC partly followed joint tracks to London Marylebone. It was a magnificent railway; but the Channel tunnel was not built, and the line was run down by BR and closed in 1969.

Many difficulties faced the Main Line Steam Trust in acquiring a section of the GC, but persistence and some very imaginative fund raising finally won the day. The Trust are now planning to extend services to Birstall in the northern suburbs of Leicester, and this additional section will provide a main line eight miles long.

Loughborough Central station has been transformed to its former importance. A splendid three-road locomotive shed has been built to the north of the station providing 12,500 sq. ft of covered accommodation; Loughborough signal box is being restored to full operational order, and the attractive GC stations along the route have been renovated. The line passes through typical Leicestershire hunting country and crosses the beautiful reservoir at Swithland by means of an impressive viaduct.

A number of large express passenger type steam locomotives are based at Loughborough, and one exciting project is the restoration to full working order of the ultimate British Pacific No. 71000 'Duke of Gloucester'. This unique engine, built in 1954 and withdrawn in 1962, had a short but distinguished career. BR decided against preserving the engine and instead removed one cylinder and a set of Caprotti valve gear for sectioned display in the Science Museum at Kensington. She arrived at the Barry scrapyard in 1967 and remained rotting away for six years until purchased by the Duke of Gloucester Steam Locomotive Trust in 1973.

Other racehorses at Loughborough include two more three-cylinder engines: rebuilt Bulleid Pacific 34039 'Boscastle' and 'Jubilee' 5690 'Leander'. In the modern two–cylinder range are three celebrated mixed-traffic 4–6–0 types whose comparable performances were avidly debated during the final years of the steam age. The engines are ex-LMS 'Black 5' 5231 '3rd (Volunteer) Battalion, The Worcestershire and Sherwood Foresters Regiment'; ex-LNER BIs 61264 and 1306 'Mayflower'—resplendent in apple-green livery—and Great Western 'Hall' 6990 'Witherslack Hall'. More main-line engines are expected in the near future.

Ex-LMS 'Jubilee' Class 5690 'Leander' giving brake-van rides at Dinting prior to her transfe to the Main Line Steam Trust at Loughborough.

Authenticity is provided by Great Central 'Director' Class 4–4–0 'Butler Henderson' on loan from BR and sadly the only surviving Great Central passenger engine. Also from the LNER stable comes the Gresley Society's hefty 'N2' Class 0–6–2 suburban tank; this engine was active on passenger trains during 1978.

One foreign locomotive adds a continental flavour: the delightful Norwegian Mogul 'King Haakon VII', regularly employed in active service. Among the smaller engines is a chunky Manning Wardle 0–6–0ST named 'Littleton' which is also used in main-line service, but diminutive engines such as the ex-North Eastern 'Y7' Class 0–4–0 ST and the 'Sentinel' 0–4–0 VBGT are for yard operations only.

CADEBY LIGHT RAILWAY

HQ and Location
Cadeby Rectory, Cadeby, Hinckley, Leicestershire. Cadeby is situated on the west side of the A447 road between Hinckley and Coalville. Market Bosworth 2 miles. Hinckley 5 miles.

Track Route
Through the Rectory grounds. Gauge: 2 ft.

Times of Opening
Operates during the afternoon of the second Saturday of each month from April to November.

Further Information from
Rev. E. R. Boston, Cadeby Rectory, Cadeby, Hinckley, Leics. Tel: Market Bosworth 290462.

It is a recognized coincidence that churchmen are often railway enthusiasts, and Cadeby more than proves the point. The Reverend E. R. (Teddy) Boston has built a 2 ft gauge line around the picturesque grounds of his rectory. The principal engine is 'Pixie', a standard Bagnall 0–4–0ST which spent its working life on the Northamptonshire Ironfield until purchased in 1962 by the Reverend Boston.

Cadeby is probably the world's smallest narrow-gauge railway, but despite being only 50 yards in length it has a station at either end of the line. Two other steam locomotives are present: a Hunslet 0–4–0ST named 'Margaret' and an Orenstein and Koppel 0–4–0WT.

In addition to the railway, visitors can enjoy a steam museum containing a turn-of-the-century Aveling Porter steamroller and a splendid 1927 Foster traction engine. Also in the grounds is a large shed housing a model layout based on the Great Western Railway with some fifty locomotives. (Trains on this system often run to a carefully planned timetable.)

Cadeby Rectory is traditionally an open house for enthusiasts, whether they come to work on the exhibits or merely to enjoy them. Often after a day's steam up enthusiasts repair to the rectory for films, transparencies, conversation, and fish and chips. The rectory also contains a noteworthy railway library. Everything that Teddy has created at Cadeby is freely shared: no charges are made (though a collection box is provided for contributions towards church restorations and locomotive fuel).

The Reverend Boston obviously has many church duties to fulfil, and it is advisable to visit during the monthly steam up. Failing this, intending visitors are requested to telephone in advance.

SHACKERSTONE AND BOSWORTH RAILWAY

HQ and Location	Shackerstone Station, Nr Market Bosworth, Leicestershire. Take the A444 Nuneaton—Burton-on-Trent road and turn right at Twycross; follow unclassified road through Congerstone.
Track Route	Shackerstone—Market Bosworth (2¾ miles). Gauge: Standard.
Times of Opening	Weekends and Bank Holidays from Easter to end of October.
Further Information from	Shackerstone Railway Society, Shackerstone Station, Shackerstone, Nr Market Bosworth, Nuneaton, Warwickshire.

The Shackerstone and Bosworth Railway runs over part of the old Ashby and Nuneaton Joint Railway opened in 1873. After it was abandoned by BR in 1970 part of the line was used by the Shackerstone Railway Society as their headquarters, and purchase of the section between Shackerstone and Shenton was effected with the aid of the associate company York Caravan Equipments Ltd. At present trains terminate at the pleasant Leicestershire town of Market Bosworth, but the society intends to extend services over the

1. The Talyllyn Railway's veteran 0–4–0ST 'Sir Haydn', built by Hughes of Loughborough in 1878, approaches Abergynolwyn.

2. *A fine preservation scene on the Stour Valley Railway at Chappel & Wakes Colne Station, Essex. Featuring ex-Southern 'S15' Class 4–6–0 No. 30841 'Greene King' with ex-LNER 'N7' Class 0–6–2T No. 69621.*

3. The LMS Stanier 'Black 5' 4–6–0 is one of the most famous locomotive classes in the world. Here we see No. 45212 hard at work on the Keighley & Worth Valley Railway.

4. Adams Radial 4–4–2T No. 488 attacks Bluebell Railway's Freshfield bank.
5. Ex-LMS 'Jinty' 0–6–0T No. 47383 erupts glorious palls of smoke as she heads a passenger train along the Severn Valley line.

6. 'David', an Andrew Barclay 0–4–0ST, delights the visitors to Steamtown, Carnforth with a ride in an old 20-ton Great Western 'Toad' brakevan.

7. *Ivatt 2–6–2T 41241 hastens along the Keighley & Worth Valley line.*
8. *'Sir Thomas', built in 1918, is a member of a well-known class of industrial
0–6–0Ts from Hudswell Clarke of Leeds. The scene is Quainton.*

9. Old Lancashire and Yorkshire Railway 0–6–0 52044 pilots Ivatt 2–6–2T
41241 along the Keighley & Worth Valley line.
10. '9F' 2–10–0 'Black Prince' climbs Dilton Marsh bank with a railtour.

11. Hunslet Austerity type 0–6–0ST 'Fred' at work on the Keighley & Worth Valley Railway. The Austerities are the most numerous preserved locomotive type in the world.

12. Class '*J52*' 0–6–0ST No. 1247—an old Great Northern shunting engine—
heads a passenger train over the North Yorkshire Moors Railway. She is seen
between Beckhole and Goathland.

13. *A 2ft gauge 0–4–0WT on the Hollycombe Woodland Railway.*
14. *The Sittingbourne & Kemsley Railway's 0–4–2ST 'Premier'.*

15. Neilson 0–4–0ST 'Alfred Padget' on the Chasewater Light Railway.
16. Snowdon Mountain Railway No. 7, 'Aylwyn', heads for the summit.

17. *Two famous LNER engines running in tandem near Leeds. V2 'Green Arrow' pilots A3 'Flying Scotsman' on a railtour comprised of vintage coaching stock.*

19. *The Main Line Steam Trust's Norwegian 2-6-0 'King Haakon VII', built in 1919, heads southwards from Loughborough along the old Great Central main line. (Right)*

18. *A French four-cylinder compound 4–6–0 of 1911 hauling a Norwegian coach and ex-Southern Railway electric stock in East Anglia! Just one of the many delights to be found on the Nene Valley Railway.*

20. *Great Western glory. An evening scene on the Severn Valley Railway with 4–6–0 7819 'Hinton Manor' heading a train of cream and brown coaches towards Bewdley.*

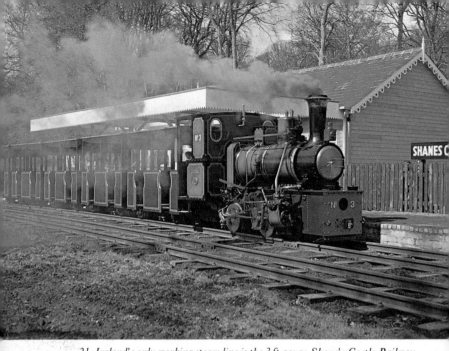

21. Ireland's only working steam line is the 3 ft gauge Shane's Castle Railway operated by the Lord O'Neill at Antrim, Northern Ireland. One of his star performers is 0–4–0WT No. 3 'Shane', built by Andrew Barclay in 1949.

23. With brass dome gleaming, *South Eastern & Chatham Class 'P' 0-6-0T No. 27 passes Holywell on the Bluebell Railway. Built in 1910, her old BR number was 31027.*

22. *The Bicton Woodland Railway operate this charming 1 ft 6 in. gauge Avonside 0-4-0T named 'Woolwich'. The engine was originally built for the Woolwich Royal Arsenal.* (Left)

24. *LMS Fairburn type 2–6–4T 2085 on the Lakeside & Haverthwaite Railway.*

25. *Restored ex-LMS 'Jubilee' 5690 'Leander' conjures up memories of the 'good old days' as she dashes through Malvern with a railtour.*

26. *A lovely scene on the Llanberis Lake Railway. The engine is 'Elidir', an 0–4–0ST built by Hunslet as long ago as 1889.*

27. *Bagnall 0–4–0ST 'Hawarden' climbs the Foxfield Railway.*

28. *Vigorous action over the North Yorkshire Moors with North Eastern Railway 0–6–0 2392 (BR Class 'J27') piloting No. 29, the ex-Lambton Railway 0–6–2T built by Kitson of Leeds in 1904.*

29. *A close-up study of the old Lambton Colliery 0–6–2T No. 29 as she awaits her turn of duty at Grosmont on the North Yorkshire Moors Railway.*

30. *North Yorkshire Moors' 'P3' Class 0–6–0 2392.*

31. *One of Bressingham's many attractions is the passenger-carrying 'Nursery Railway' built to a gauge of 1 ft 11½ in.*

32. *0–4–0ST 'Sir Cecil A. Cochrane' on the Tanfield Railway.*

33. *Autumnal colours on the 2 ft gauge Leighton Buzzard Narrow Gauge Railway. The engine is P. C. Allen, a 1912-built Orenstein & Koppel 0-4-0WT rescued from Spain by Sir Peter Allen.*

34. LNER A4 'Sir Nigel Gresley' with the 'Bulmer's Cider' Pullman train at the Bulmer Steam Centre, Hereford.

35. 'Hamburg', a 75-year-old 0–6–0T from Hudswell Clarke of Leeds, raises the echoes as she battles with adverse grades near Oakworth on the Keighley & Worth Valley line.

36. *The pastoral beauty of the Kent & East Sussex line makes a fine setting for Norwegian Mogul No. 19, seen heading a rake of Maunsell bogie coaches.*

37. *North Norfolk Railway's Peckett 0–6–0ST 'John D. Hammer'.*

38. The Ffestiniog Railway's celebrated 'Blanche'—a Hunslet 2–4–0ST tender of 1893—heads an up morning train with Moelwyn Bach to the rear.

39. *The plaque carried by LNER A4 'Mallard' commemorating that engine's epic record-breaking 126 mph dash down Stoke Bank over forty years ago.*
40. *The nameplate of Dinting Railway Centre's famous 'Jubilee' 5596.*

additional one-and-a-half miles to Shenton Station which is situated on the site where the Battle of Bosworth was fought by Richard III and Henry VII in 1485. (The site is now open to the public.)

The Shackerstone and Bosworth Railway runs close to the Ashby Canal, opened in 1804 to convey coal from the Leicester Field to the manufacturing areas of England. A network of tramways once connected the collieries with the canal, and the coal was carried in 70 ft long narrow boats. Old rivalries between railway and canal are now atoned, and the society, in co-operation with the Ashby Canal Association, hopes to offer combined rail/canal trips.

At time of writing, all the locomotives assembled at Shackerstone are of the industrial type, the oldest being 'The King', an 0–4–0 Well Tank built by E. Borrows and Sons of St Helens, Lancashire, in 1906. The most unusual is No. 11, a unique Hunslet 0–4–0ST specially built in 1925 to pass beneath a low bridge at a Nottinghamshire colliery. This engine is squat in appearance and cabless—a feature not appreciated by Shackerstone's crews in wet weather! Also among the smaller engines is the delightful Peckett 0–4–0ST 'Herbert', a member of that builder's 'Yorktown' design.

On the heavier side comes No. 21, a standard 16 in. cylinder 0–6–0ST from Hawthorn Leslie of Newcastle-upon-Tyne in 1938. This engine was the last working survivor of a set which once operated at the Stewarts and Lloyds steel works at Corby.

Providing the ultimate in power are Nos. 3 and 4, a couple of superb heavy-duty side tanks from Robert Stephenson and Hawthorn. Built in 1949 and 1951, these 50-ton trojans can haul 1,000-ton trains; their class was designed for power stations. They came from Nechells Power Station in Birmingham.

In addition to the steam locomotives an interesting collection of rolling stock, traction engines and steamrollers can also be seen.

BIRMINGHAM RAILWAY MUSEUM

HQ and Location The Steam Depot, Warwick Road, Tyseley, Birmingham 11. The depot

	is located off the A41 Warwick Road, some three miles from Birmingham City Centre. Buses from Bull Ring Bus Station, Birmingham (book to Reddings Lane, Tyseley).
Gauge	Standard.
Times of Opening	Sunday afternoons. Special steaming days between June and October—as advertised in the railway press.
Further Information from	The Standard Gauge Steam Trust, The Steam Depot, Warwick Road, Tyseley, Birmingham 11.

Apart from its selection of locomotives, the former Great Western depot at Tyseley is one of Britain's principal steam maintenance centres; the well-equipped workshop includes a huge wheel lathe, a wheel drop pit and an ex-BR crane for lifting out engine boilers during overhauls. Tyseley is situated on the old GW main line between Paddington and Chester. The depot has facilities for watering, coaling and turning, and thus attracts visiting railtour engines—especially from the GW stud at Didcot.

Tyseley's thirteen resident locomotives are predominantly GW but the most celebrated are 7029 'Clun Castle' and ex-LMS 'Jubilee' 5593 'Kolhapur'. Over the final years of steam 'Clun Castle' became a much loved railtour engine and worked the last steam train from Paddington in 1965. In the previous year she made a record run from Plymouth to Bristol, during which she reached 96 mph and maintained 90 mph for twelve miles continuously. She was also the last steam locomotive to leave Birmingham (Snow Hill) with a passenger train. 'Clun Castle' was actually built under BR auspices in 1950, one of a batch of GW Castles whose construction had been delayed by World War II. 'Kolhapur' is another Tyseley engine of long standing, now beautifully restored in authentic LMS red.

Three other Castles are at Tyseley: 5043 'Earl of Mount Edgcumbe'; 5080 'Defiant', and 7027 'Thornbury Castle'. All were rescued from Barry. Numbers 5080 and 7027 will eventually be restored as working companions to 'Clun Castle' but, sadly, 5043 will be used as a vital source of spare parts and will never run again.

The Castles are in the good company of several other GW classes: 4983 'Albert Hall' (bearing a boiler once carried by a Saint); two '57XX' Pannier Tanks purchased from London Transport; a '96XX' Pannier Tank; a '56XX' Class 0–6–2T and a '41XX' 2–6–2T—a standard suburban passenger engine. Two Peckett 0–4–0STs complete the collection along with several Pullman coaches.

Tyseley's development continues in conjunction with the West Midlands Metropolitan County Council and Birmingham City Council, and future plans include a platform and station for the steam site area, a carriage shed, a museum and a two-road loco shed of standard GW styling (the original roundhouse was demolished during the 1960s).

Open days at Tyseley are always well attended. Several engines are put into steam, and there are additional, visiting engines working in on railtours.

Situated close to the National Exhibition Centre, Tyseley railway museum seems sure of a thriving future.

BULMER RAILWAY CENTRE

HQ and Location	Bulmer Railway Centre, Whitecross Road, Hereford. The site is located half-a-mile from the city centre on the A438 Brecon Road on the premises of Bulmer's Cider Factory. Access to the centre and car park from Whitecross Road.
Gauge	Standard.
Times of Opening	Weekend afternoons from April to September. Steam-hauled brake-van rides on last Sunday in each month; principal steaming days on Easter and Spring Bank Holidays and other special weekends.

Further Information from

The Visitors' Secretary, Bulmer Railway Centre, 18 Hinton Crescent, Hereford, HR2 6AE.

This centre was established in 1968 by H. P. Bulmer, the Hereford cider makers, as a depot for the Bulmer Cider Train and ex-GWR locomotive 6000, 'King George V'. The centre is operated on behalf of Bulmer by Steam in Hereford Ltd (the '6000 Locomotive Association').

'King George V' was withdrawn in 1962 after running some two million miles in thirty-five years of active service. Although originally destined for the Great Western Museum at Swindon, Bulmer offered to undertake complete restoration of the engine to main-line order, on condition that she be based at Hereford as a working exhibit. However, after British Rail's last steam locomotives were withdrawn in 1968 a ban was imposed on steam specials and remained until 1971 when, to the nation's delight, 'King George V' undertook a successful week-long railtour with the Pullman Cider Train, comprised of former Golden Arrow and Bourne-

Record-breaking LMS Princess Royal Pacific 6201 'Princess Elizabeth' bursts under a bridge near Church Stretton with the Midland Jubilee Special.

mouth Belle stock. This historic run set a precedent for steam railtours. Four of the Pullman coaches are named after the wives of Bulmer directors.

The Bulmer centre forms a working depot for steam railtours over the now famous route between Newport and Shrewsbury, and several other preservation societies have brought their engines to participate in the centre's activities and main-line running. Notable among these is the Princess Elizabeth Locomotive Society with Stanier LMS Pacific 6201 'Princess Elizabeth', and the Merchant Navy Locomotive Preservation Society with ex-Southern Railway Bulleid Pacific 35028 'Clan Line'. On open days at least two of them are in steam.

'Princess Elizabeth' was saved from the scrapyard in 1962, and the society was formed to restore her to main-line order. After years of toil their efforts were rewarded in 1976 when an invitation was received from British Rail to include 6201 in the approved list of engines for special railtours. Her first trip was on 5 June 1976—exactly a hundred years after the birth of William Stanier. On the footplate was R. A. Riddles, the man responsible for producing BR's standard steam designs during the early 1950s. Riddles had supervised footplate operations during 6201's epic test run between London and Glasgow in 1936. Now restored to her original LMS Crimson Lake livery, 'Princess Elizabeth' is exactly as she was when built forty-six years ago.

'Clan Line' was withdrawn in July 1967 after ending her days on Britain's last steam-hauled expresses between London and Weymouth. She was purchased for preservation the following month. In 1975 she arrived at Hereford and took part—along with 'Princess Elizabeth'—in the Shildon Parade. In recent years she has been a popular railtour engine.

Other engines at the Bulmer Railway Centre are Great Western 0-6-0 Pannier Tank 5786, purchased from London Transport, and 'Carnarvon', a Kitson 0-6-0ST from Corby Ironstone Mines; both of these engines belong to the Worcester Locomotive Society.

Peckett 0-4-0ST 'Pectin' owned by the 6000 Locomotive Association is invariably the engine chosen to give rides around the centre, and the sight of this lovely red Saddle Tank hauling a 20-ton Great Western 'Toad' brake van is characteristic of the centre.

SEVERN VALLEY RAILWAY

HQ and Location

Bridgnorth Railway Station, Bridgnorth, Salop. Bridgnorth is situated on the A442 from Kidderminster to Wellington. Nearest BR stations: Wolverhampton for Bridgnorth (13 miles); Kidderminster for Bewdley (3 miles). Midland Red buses connect from BR stations to the Severn Valley.

Track Route

Bridgnorth—Foley Park (14½ miles). Gauge: Standard.

Times of Opening

Weekends from March to October; most Tuesdays, Wednesdays and Thursdays from May to mid-July; daily from mid-July to early September; Bank Holidays.

Further Information from

The General Manager, The Railway Station, Bewdley, Worcestershire, DY12 1BG. Tel: Bewdley 403816 and 400073. Travel Enquiries: The Railway Station, Bridgnorth, Salop, WV16 5DT. Tel: Bridgnorth 4361.

The Severn Valley Railway is Britain's preservationists' 'premier line'; it has almost fifteen route miles, over thirty locomotives, fifty-five coaches and some sixty goods wagons—many excitingly restored to their private-owner condition. The railway is supported by a seven-thousand-strong membership association, and restoration work is carried out at Bridgnorth and Bewdley. Enthusiasts' Days are nationally famous, with twelve engines in steam and five trains in continuous operation.

The original Severn Valley Railway was opened in 1862; it was forty miles long and linked Hartlebury with Shrewsbury to provide a direct route between Shrewsbury and Worcester. It was in-

An old-time freight train trundles along between the passenger trains on the Severn Valley Railway. Ex-GW '5700' Class 0–6–0PT No. 5764 provides the motive power.

corporated into the Great Western Railway in 1872, and a line was later built to connect Kidderminster and Bewdley, enabling trains to run from the West Midlands to Shrewsbury via the Severn Valley.

Closed under Beeching in 1963, the line seemed destined to fade into history, but in 1965 the Severn Valley Railway Society raised 10 per cent of the £25,000 needed to purchase the five-mile section from Bridgnorth to Aveley. Later that year Collet 0–6–0 No. 3205 arrived on the railway, and by 1970 trains ran again between Bridgnorth and Hampton Loade.

Under the chairmanship of the late Sir Gerald Nabarro a further £110,000 was raised for purchase of the railway from Avebury through Bewdley to Foley Park, Kidderminster, and in 1974 services were extended to Bewdley. The remaining two miles to Foley Park has yet to be opened on a regular basis, but this extension provides valuable access to British Rail and will eventually enable through trains to run from Kidderminster to Bridgnorth. Beyond Bridgnorth parts of the former track bed have been sold, and Severn Valley trains will never reach Shrewsbury again.

The Severn Valley Railway closely follows the river's meandering course and is a delightful line to travel over. Trains run at ninety-minute intervals, but are increased to a forty-five-minute frequency during peak times. During the fifty-minute journey from Bridgnorth the railway encounters a succession of cuttings, embankments, viaducts and tunnels. Hampton Loade, four-and-a-half miles from Bridgnorth, is popular with fishermen and has a ferry crossing the river. Next the train passes Aveley, where a colliery was active until 1969. A steep climb to a summit is followed by the descent to Highley, which is approached by a superb curve. Two miles further on is the picturesque station at Arley; then the line crosses Victoria Bridge, with fine views of the river far below. Trimpley Reservoir next appears on the right hand side, usually dotted with coloured sailing dinghies. After a run through deeply wooded country, historic Bewdley is approached over a high sandstone viaduct, the railway commanding a panoramic view. (Bewdley is noted for its wildlife park.)

The Severn Valley's engines are wonderfully varied and include several unique examples. One of the most interesting is the Stanier 'Crab' 2–6–0 2968 built at Crewe in 1934—Stanier's first design as Chief Mechanical Engineer of the LMS. The only LNER engine represented is 3442 'The Great Marquess', one of Gresley's three-cylinder 'K4' 2–6–0s built for the West Highland line from Glasgow to Fort William and Mallaig.

A very popular engine is 'Gordon', one of Riddles' War Department 2–10–0s built in readiness for the European Invasion in 1943. These engines were Britain's first 2–10–0s. Also associated with war-time operations is LMS '8F' 2–8–0 8233 owned by the Stanier 8F Society. Built by the North British in 1940, this locomotive became LMS No. 8233. Later she was incorporated into War Department stock and subsequently shipped to Persia. She returned home in 1952 and, after some years on the Longmoor Military Railway, was taken into BR stock in 1957 as number 48773. The engine was withdrawn from service in July 1968, but had received heavy repairs at Crewe Works in 1966 and was an ideal example to select for preservation. A closely related engine—Stanier 'Black 5' 4–6–0 45110 'Biggin Hill'—is also hard at work on the railway; another 'Black 5', No. 45000, is on loan from the National Railway Museum.

In 1978 the Severn Valley Railway made preservation history when BR Standard Pacific 70000 'Britannia' was finally restored to full working order and put into steam. The engine's designer, R. A. Riddles, unveiled the nameplates.

Many Great Western locomotives can be seen including 4930 'Hagley Hall', 6960 'Raveningham Hall' and 7819 'Hinton Manor'. Others include a '28XX' 2–8–0, Collett 0–6–0 No. 3205, a range of 2–6–2Ts and several Pannier Tanks. The motive power roster is completed by a stud of industrial engines, along with ex-LMS 'Jinty' 47383, which takes its turn on passenger duties.

CHASEWATER LIGHT RAILWAY

HQ and Location	Chasewater Pleasure Park, Nr Brownhills, Staffordshire. Chasewater is situated on the north side of the A5 (Watling Street) just west of Brownhills. Entrance along Pool Road. Wolverhampton 10 miles.
Track Route	Alongside Chasewater (2 miles). Gauge: Standard.
Times of Opening	Steaming on second and fourth Sundays each month from April to September; Bank Holiday Sundays and Mondays during the season.
Further Information from	Railway Preservation Society, Chasewater Light Railway, Chasewater Pleasure Park, Nr Brownhills, Staffs. Tel: 021 523 8516.

Chasewater is a large canal reservoir popularly used for sailing, power boat races and water skiing, and the railway is now an in-

Chasewater Light Railway's 0–4–0ST 'Asbestos', built by Hawthorn Leslie in 1909, shuffle along its six-wheeled coach from the Manchester Sheffield and Lincolnshire Railway.

tegral part of a rapidly expanding Pleasure Park. The two-mile line follows the lake and actually crosses it over a narrow causeway a quarter of a mile long. Eventually stations will be situated at either end of the line. The railway serves as a permanent reminder of the long tradition of coal and railways in industrial Staffordshire.

The Chasewater Light Railway is controlled by the Chasewater Railway Society, previously known as the Railway Preservation Society—a group formed in 1959 as part of a national movement to preserve historic relics from Britain's railways (and a founder-member of the Association of Railway Preservation Societies).

The line was built in 1856 as part of the Cannock Chase and Wolverhampton Railway and until its closure in 1960 it provided access to several collieries. The RPS acquired the line on a long-term lease from the National Coal Board, and the Chasewater Light Railway was formed to operate trains under licence from the society. Visitors can also see a museum of beautifully restored small relics collected by society members over many years.

The Chasewater Railway has the oldest working steam loco-motive in the Midlands: the redoubtable 'Alfred Paget' built in

1882 by Neilson. It is sad that the Cannock Chase and Wolver-hampton Railway's Beyer Peacock 0–4–2ST 'McClean', built for the railway in its opening year, could not have been saved.

Perhaps the most familiar engine in recent years has been Haw-thorn Leslie 0–4–0ST 'Asbestos', attractively decked in maroon livery. Another arrival to the line was an 0–4–0 VBGT 'Sentinel' which once worked for the West Midlands Gas Board. The railway has eight steam locomotives and all are of industrial design.

Steam-operated push-and-pull trains work the system using the ex-BR 'diesel multiple unit' trailer coach—an amazing combina-tion, especially when the Neilson Pug is at the business end. An interesting collection of rolling stock is on display, the most note-worthy item being the Maryport and Carlisle Railway six-wheeled coach, which was built in 1875 and is now the only surviving relic from this railway. Other stock includes an 1890-built Manchester Sheffield and Lincolnshire six-wheeled coach and a London and North Western travelling post office sorting van of 1909.

FOXFIELD LIGHT RAILWAY

HQ and Location	Foxfield Colliery, Dilhorne, Blythe Bridge, Nr Stoke-on-Trent, Staf-fordshire. Blythe Bridge is situated on the main A50 Derby–Stoke road. For Foxfield leave the A50 at Blythe Marsh and follow the A521 turning on to unclassified roads for Dilhorne and Foxfield. Stoke 9 miles.
Track Route	Foxfield–Blythe Bridge ($3\frac{1}{2}$ miles). Gauge: Standard.
Times of Opening	Sundays from April to September; special trains at other times by arrangement.
Further Information from	Foxfield Light Railway Society, Foxfield Colliery, Dilhorne, Blythe Bridge, Nr Stoke, Staffs. Tel: Uttoxeter 4669.

'J. T. Daly'—a Bagnall 0–4–0ST, built in 1931, climbs away from Foxfield with a train ▸ *Blythe Bridge. The passenger vehicle is an ex-Midland Railway scenery van.*

This rural undulating line was built in 1893 by the owners of Fox-field Colliery to convey their coal to a connection with the North Staffordshire Railway at Blythe Bridge. The line remained in use until closed by the National Coal Board in 1965, after which the colliery and railway were purchased by Tean Minerals Ltd. This company now processes minerals in the colliery buildings, but the original idea to bring in the stones by railway was abandoned, and the company leased the line to the Foxfield Railway Society in 1966. All the original engines had been displaced, and the society began to build up their own stock along with privately owned exhibits.

As the trains leave Foxfield they face a spectacular climb with a short stretch of 1-in-22, easing to 1-in-30 for half-a-mile until the summit is reached in a small wood. In coal-carrying days, loaded wagons were brought up to this summit five at a time and assembled into full train loads for the down-hill journey on to Blythe Bridge. Today the society often use two engines up to the summit, 750 ft above sea level. During the journey to Blythe Bridge passengers gain views of 17th-century Stansmore Hall and 13th century Caverswall Castle.

Fourteen steam locomotives can be seen on the railway, and appropriately all are of the industrial type with 0–4–0/0–6–0 Saddle Tanks predominating. An exception is 0–4–0 Crane Tank 'Roker' built by Robert Stephenson and Hawthorn in 1940 for Doxford's Wearside shipyard. Another unusual engine is No. 1—a little 0–4–0 'Fireless' built by Andrew Barclay in 1930.

Rolling stock includes four ex-LMS bogie scenery vans, two converted into observation coaches. Former LMS and BR bogie coaches are also used, and an interesting selection of pre-grouping wagons is on view. A Smith-Rodley steam crane completes the items to be seen on this delightful railway.

DINTING RAILWAY CENTRE

HQ and Location	Dinting Railway Centre, Dinting Lane, Dinting, Glossop, Nr Manchester. The centre is situated off the A57 Manchester–Sheffield road. Manchester 12 miles. Glossop 1 mile. BR services run from Manchester Piccadilly to Dinting, Mondays to Saturdays. Access to the centre is from Dinting BR station.
Gauge	Standard.
Times of Opening	Every weekend and most weekdays. Steaming on Sundays and Bank Holidays from early March until the end of October.
Further Information from	Dinting Railway Centre, Dinting Lane, Dinting, Glossop, Nr Manchester. Tel: Glossop 5596.

This splendid working museum began when a group of Stockport railway enthusiasts joined together in 1967 to save Stockport (Edgeley) 'Jubilee' 45596 'Bahamas' from scrap. Secured for £3,000, the 'Jubilee' was overhauled to main-line standards by Hunslet of Leeds for a further £6,500. She then returned to Stockport for display, but owing to the depot's impending closure the five-hundred-strong Bahamas Locomotive Society had to find an alternative place to keep her.

The redundant Great Central engine shed at Dinting was purchased in 1968. Situated on the old Great Central main line it was formerly a sub-depot of Gorton, and its engines—apart from being employed on the Glossop and Waterside branches—were used to assist trains over the long 1-in-100 slog up through the Pennines to Woodhead tunnel. The depot was very derelict and overgrown. Today the ten-acre area includes a new three-track Exhibition Hall 200 ft long and 40 ft wide.

The main attraction is 'Bahamas', now restored to her LMS Crimson Lake livery and complete with the Bahamas' coat of arms on her nameplate. Built in 1935 by the North British of Glasgow, 'Bahamas' was a member of the 191-strong 'Jubilee' class but was unusual in having a double chimney experimentally fitted at Crewe in 1961. In 1969 'Bahamas' was joined at Dinting by sister LMS express passenger engine 6115 'Scots Guardsman', a noted Long-sight (Manchester) engine for many years and a member of the 'Royal Scot' Class.

In marked contrast is ex-GCR '04' Class 2–8–0 No. 102, built at Gorton in 1911 to the design of the Great Central's Chief Mechanical Engineer J. G. Robinson. For half a century these 2–8–0s worked heavy trains over the entire Great Central system, and were characteristic performers over the lonely expanse of the Pennines between Manchester and Sheffield. The type also saw extensive use abroad during both world wars. The engine is on loan from the National Railway Museum.

Another engine on loan is ex-LNWR 0–6–2T Coal Tank No. 1054, built at Crewe in 1888 and last survivor of a once numerous class. (Withdrawn from Abergavenny in 1958.)

Dinting is also worth a visit for its industrial engines. These include Hudswell Clarke 0–6–0T 'Nunlow', now beautifully restored in Great Central green; 0–4–0 Crane Tank 'Southwick' from Dox-

inting's Avonside 0–6–0ST provides the power for rides in the ex-North Eastern brake van.
the foreground is an old Great Central Railway water column.

ford's Wearside Shipyard and one of Beyer Peacock's famous 0–4–0 Steam Tram engines. This rare exhibit was built in 1886 and worked on the Oldham tramway system.

Set among the Pennine foothills, Dinting Railway Centre is run by the Bahamas Locomotive Society as a registered Educational Charity. Footplate rides and brake van journeys are available on steaming days, and an added attraction to the full-sized engines is the 900 ft long model railway built to 5 in. and $3\frac{1}{2}$ in. gauge by the Buxton Model Engineering Society. This railway also carries passengers.

Dinting's tracks connect up with British Rail, and the centre provides the north-west with a valuable stabling and maintenance point for preserved locomotives.

Area 6. Wales

PENRHYN CASTLE INDUSTRIAL RAILWAY MUSEUM

HQ and Location	Penrhyn Castle Museum, Nr Bangor, Gwynedd. Penrhyn Castle is one mile east of Bangor, reached from the A5 road. Nearest BR station: Bangor.
Gauge	1 ft $11\frac{1}{2}$ in.; 3 ft; 4 ft; Standard.
Times of Opening	Daily from April to October.
Further Information from	Penrhyn Castle Museum, Nr Bangor, Gwynedd, LL57 4HN. Tel: Bangor (0248) 53084.

This museum—formed in 1963 by the National Trust—is largely devoted to the railways which once served the vast slate industry of North Wales. Housed in the large stables at Penrhyn Castle, the museum falls into three principal groups: the Penrhyn Railway Collection, the Dinorwic Collection and General Exhibits.

The Penrhyn engines are of 1 ft $11\frac{1}{2}$ in. gauge, and the two locomotives 'Charles' and 'Hugh Napier' are both Hunslet 0–4–0STs built in 1882 and 1904 respectively. The former was a Penrhyn main-line engine with inside cylinders of 10 in. diameter; the latter is a member of the Hunslet 'Quarry' class and spent her working life on a mountainside above Bethesda.

From Dinorwic Quarries is the amazing 4ft gauge frameless 0–4–0 'Fire Queen' built in 1848 by Horlock of North Fleet Iron Works, Kent. Along with a sister engine, 'Fire Queen' worked the Padarn Railway until the 1880s. Despite her ungainly appearance this engine is of sound design and embodies several features which were in advance of their time.

Holyhead

Penrhyn Castle Museum
Bangor
Penllyn *Llanberis Lake Rly*
Llanberis
Caernarvon *Snowdon Mountain Rly*
Snowdon Wrexham
Festiniog Rly Blaenau Ffestiniog
Porthmadog Bala
Bala Lake Rly
Llanuwchllyn
Barmouth
Barmouth Ferry Nant Gwernol
Fairbourne
Fairbourne Rly Llanfair
Caereinion Welshpool *Welshpool &*
Tywyn *Talyllyn Rly* Sylfaen *Llanfair Rly*

Vale of Rheidol Rly
Aberystwyth
Devil's Bridge

Cardigan

Bronwydd Arms *Gwili Rly* Brecon
Carmarthen

Pembroke
Swansea

Cardiff

AREA 6

WALES

GWYNEDD CLWYD POWYS DYFED
GWENT GLAMORGAN ANGLESEY

Among the general exhibits is a 3 ft gauge 0–4–0 Vertical Boiler engine built by De Winton of Caernarvon in 1893 and employed at Penmaenmawr Granite Quarries. Of the same gauge is a lovely little Black Hawthorn 0–4–0ST of 1885 which ran as 'Kettering Furnaces No. 3'. The oldest standard-gauge engine is 'Haydock', built by Robert Stephenson in 1879. This centenarian spent much of her working life at Haydock Foundry, St Helens, Lancs.

In addition to the locomotives, the museum contains early rolling stock and track relating to various slate railways, and a number of models and small exhibits, including a Victorian 4 ft gauge rail cycle used by an engineer for track-inspection purposes.

LLANBERIS LAKE RAILWAY

HQ and Location	Gilfach Ddu Station, Llanberis, Gwynedd, North Wales. Llanberis is situated on the A4086 Caernarvon-Betws-y-Coed road. Caernarvon 7 miles. Nearest BR station: Bangor; then by bus to Llanberis, either direct or via Caernarvon.
Track Route	Llanberis–Penllyn (2 miles). Gauge: 1 ft 11½ in.
Times of Opening	Daily from the end of May until the beginning of October.
Further Information from	The General Manager, Llanberis Lake Railway, Llanberis, Caernarvon. LL55 4TY. Tel: Llanberis 549.

The Llanberis Lake Railway was opened in 1971 and follows part of the trackbed of the former 4 ft gauge Padarn Railway, which carried slate from the Dinorwic Quarries at Llanberis up to Port Dinorwic on the Menai Straits. The quarries finally closed in 1969, and the Llanberis Lake Railway was formed as a commercial enterprise to create work for former quarry employees and to preserve certain aspects of the industry. The Dinorwic Slate Company's old workshops are situated near to Gilfach Ddu station, and the National Museum of Wales has converted these buildings into a quarry museum and opened them to the public.

Three of the Llanberis Lake Railway's engines—'Elidir', 'Wild Aster' and 'Dolbadarn'—came from the Dinorwic Quarries. Painted in bright red livery, these engines are standard 'Quarry' Hunslet 0–4–0STs and once worked on the mountainside ledges from which the slate was taken. Their building dates are 1889, 1904 and 1922 respectively. The two other engines at Llanberis are both of German origin. One is a Henschel 0–4–0T named 'Helen Kathryn', and the other a Jung 0–4–0WT of 1937 named 'Ginette Marie'—built to a standard German design for quarry shunting.

From Gilfach Ddu the railway follows the east shore of the lake and provides travellers with some of the finest lake and mountain scenery in Wales. Llanberis village is visible across the water, and there are exciting views of the Snowdon Mountain Range, including the summit itself.

On the outward journey trains pass through the intermediate station and passing point of Cei Llydan and proceed direct to Penllyn (the end of the lake). Passengers are not allowed to leave or join the train at Penllyn owing to narrow clearances. On the return journey trains stop at Cei Llydan where there are excellent picnic sites beneath the trees or on the shore of the lake.

SNOWDON MOUNTAIN RAILWAY

HQ and Location	Llanberis, Gwynedd, North Wales. Llanberis is situated on the A4086 Caernarvon–Betws-y-Coed road. Caernarvon 7 miles. Nearest BR station: Bangor; then by bus to Llanberis, either direct or via Caernarvon.
Track Route	Llanberis–Mt Snowdon summit ($4\frac{3}{4}$ miles). Gauge: 2 ft $7\frac{1}{2}$ in.
Times of Opening	From Easter to the beginning of October.

Further Information from

The General Manager, Snowdon Mountain Railway Ltd, Llanberis, Gwynedd, North Wales, LL55 4TY. Tel: Llanberis 223.

The Snowdon Mountain Railway has maintained continuous steam operation since opened in 1896, and is thus not a 'preserved' line in the strictest sense. The line's purpose is—and always has been—to carry tourists to the 3,560 ft summit of Snowdon—the highest mountain in England and Wales. During the season old Swiss-built tank engines propel one-coach trains to the summit every half hour, and in so doing traverse maximum gradients of 1-in-5.

A journey over the line is exciting, and on a clear day the views extend across the mountains of North Wales to Anglesey, Cardigan Bay, the Isle of Man and the Wicklow Mountains of Ireland. The line is single throughout, but passing points occur at Hebron, Half-way and Clogwyn, where there is a spectacular drop of 2,000 ft to the Llanberis Pass below. During the early and late season snow and ice occasionally prevent the summit being reached, and trains

A characteristic scene on the Snowdon Mountain Railway with No. 3 'Wyddfa', one of the Swiss-built 0–4–2 rack engines, built in 1895.

terminate at Clogwyn. A restaurant and bar are situated on the summit.

The Snowdon line is Britain's only rack-and-pinion railway. Two toothed racks are set side by side in the centre of the track, and cogged wheels placed underneath the locomotives engage with the teeth and provide the driving force. This mechanism is known as the Abt System and is vital for surmounting severe gradients on which conventional smooth wheeled locomotives would slip to a standstill.

Seven 0–4–2Ts can be seen on the line, all built between 1895 and 1923 by the Swiss Locomotive Works at Winterthur. Swiss engines were chosen because of that country's experience in rack railways and locomotives.

FESTINIOG RAILWAY

HQ and Location   Harbour Station, Porthmadog, Gwynedd. Porthmadog is situated on the A487 Welsh Coast Road 20 miles south of Caernarvon. Nearest BR stations: Porthmadog for Harbour Station; Minffordd for the Festiniog Railway.

Track Route   Porthmadog–Tanygrisiau (12¼ miles). The final extension to the centre of Blaenau Ffestiniog is scheduled for completion by 1980. Gauge: 1 ft 11½ in.

Times of Opening   Weekends from mid-February to end of March; daily from end of March to early November; weekends for the remainder of November and December; Christmas Holiday Specials.

Further Information from   Festiniog Railway Society Ltd, Harbour Station, Porthmadog, Gwynedd. Tel: Porthmadog 2384.

This famous railway was built in 1836 to convey slate from the mountainsides around Blaenau Ffestiniog to the harbour at Porthmadog. Steam locomotives were introduced in 1863, and two years later passenger services commenced. In 1872 the Festiniog pioneered the use of bogie coaches in Britain.

During the 20th century slate traffic began to decline, and bus competition forced the passenger trains to resort to seasonal running only, until their complete withdrawal at the beginning of World War II. By 1946 virtually all operations on the line had ceased. For six years the run down Festiniog lay abandoned, until in 1954 a new administration took over to reinstate the line, and the Festiniog Railway Society was formed to assist on a voluntary basis.

The following year passenger services were resumed between Porthmadog and Boston Lodge, and by 1958 Tan-y-Bwlch was reached seven-and-a-half miles up the line. After a period of consolidation, trains ran to Dduallt in 1968. During the 1970s the drive towards Blaenau Ffestiniog was continued, and the line was extended further to Llyn Ystradau, and onwards to its present terminus at Tanygrisiau. Difficulties in building these upper extensions have included cutting through two-and-a-half miles of solid rock to by-pass an older section of the line flooded by the Llyn Ystradau hydro-electric scheme. The Manpower Services Commission and the Wales Tourist Board have both given grants to help. The company's intention is to reach Blaenau Ffestiniog by 1980, and a shared station for Festiniog and BR trains is being built.

The Festiniog trains cross the sea wall and begin their long climb into the hills—Blaenau Ffestiniog being some 700 ft above sea level. Passengers enjoy a breathtaking panorama of Snowdonia, with superb views of the sea and Harlech Castle. In contrast, the beautiful Dwyryd Valley is seen from a commanding position on the hillside as the train climbs to Tan-y-Bwlch. Next comes Dduallt, which has a fine view-point and picnic site. After passing through the tunnel, the train joins the newly built section alongside the lake as far as the present terminus at Tanygrisiau.

The Llechwedd Slate Caverns are situated at Blaenau Ffestiniog, and visitors can take a tram ride into a bygone age in vast under-

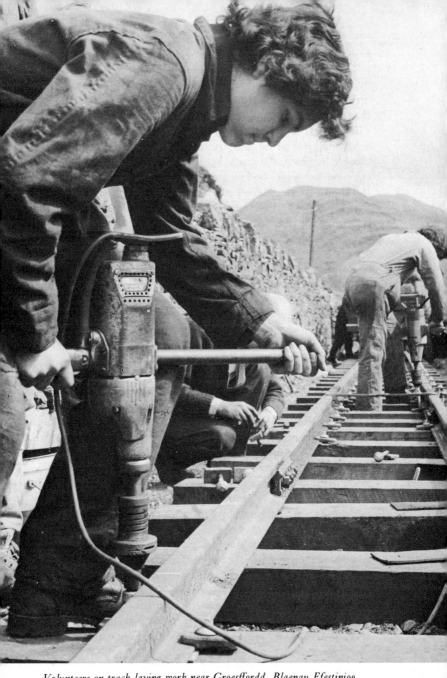

Volunteers on track-laying work near Groesffordd, Blaenau Ffestiniog

ground slate quarries with a network of tunnels and caverns.

The Festiniog's first two steam locomotives can still be seen on the line, and at time of writing they are 116 years old! Named 'Prince' and 'Princess', they were built by George England of Hatcham Iron Works, London, as 0-4-0 side tank engines with tenders. Their side tanks have since been replaced by saddle tanks.

Visitors to the Festiniog are intrigued by the famous 0-4-4-0 'double engines' designed by Robert Fairlie. These unusual engines incorporate two separate boilers with one central firebox, and appear from a distance as two engines placed back to back and facing in opposite directions. Apart from their superior power, the Fairlies are flexible on sharp curves as each engine is mounted on articulated bogies. The engine's cabs are placed centrally—the driver occuping one side and the fireman the other. The first engine of this type arrived on the Festiniog in 1869.

In 1879 and 1885 two Fairlies, named 'Merddyn Emrys' and 'Livingston Thompson' respectively, were built at the Festiniog Railway's Boston Lodge Works. The former engine was rebuilt in 1970 with a new superheated boiler, while parts of the second went into the building of a new Fairlie named 'Earl of Merioneth'. This engine was completed at Boston Lodge Works during the late 1970s.

'Blanche' and 'Linda' are both ex-Penrhyn Hunslets built in 1893. These engines are enlarged versions of Hunslet's Standard 'Quarry' Saddle Tank and have inclined cylinders. Both engines have been rebuilt into 2-4-0Ts with tenders and have proved to be extremely useful engines. During 1977 'Blanche' ran over eleven thousand miles. Another engine which has run high mileages is 'Mountaineer', an American 2-6-2T built for Army service in 1917. After ending her days on the Tramway de Pithiviers à Toury in France she was purchased by a member of the Festiniog Railway Society.

All active steam locomotives on the Festiniog Railway are equipped for oil firing, as the risk of sparks from coal burners would threaten the commercial forests planted alongside the line. Eleven locomotives can be seen on the railway. Much of the line's early coaching stock remains in use, including some original four-wheelers known as 'bug boxes'. However, new steel and aluminium coaches have been built—some as observation buffet cars.

During 1977 the Festiniog recorded 390,000 passenger journeys—the highest of any private railway in Britain. The supporting society has a membership in excess of 7,500.

BALA LAKE RAILWAY

HQ and Location	Llanuwchllyn Station, Nr Bala, Gwynedd. Llanuwchllyn is reached by turning off the A494 Dolgellau–Bala road, 5 miles south of Bala.
Track Route	Bala–Llanuwchllyn (4½ miles). Gauge: 1 ft 11½ in.
Times of Opening	Daily from mid-April to the beginning of October; weekends only during the remainder of April and October.
Further Information from	General Manager, Llanuwchllyn Station, Nr Bala, Gwynedd, LL23 7DD. Tel: Llanuwchllyn 666.

The former Great Western line from Ruabon to Barmouth was a lonely cross-country route which provided glorious views of wild terrain. One of the journey's highlights was the four-and-a-half-mile stretch which ran alongside Bala Lake.

This line closed in 1965, but in August 1972 the Bala Lake Railway opened with a stretch of narrow-gauge line laid on the standard-gauge trackbed from Llanuwchllyn to the lakeside. Since then the line has been extended to its present terminus at Bala. The Bala Lake Railway was opened for tourists, but it has also proved popular with local residents. The railway company is supported by the Bala Lake Railway Society.

Near Llanuwchllyn, visitors can see the location of the first Welsh gold mine. This was discovered by the Romans, and the site of their camp can be seen from the train. The intermediate station is Llangower, which incorporates a passing loop and operational signal box of standard-gauge proportions. Nearby is a picnic area and a safe beach for children.

Pride of the line is the red-liveried 'Maid Marion', a Quarry Hunslet 0–4–0ST of 1903 from Dinorwic Slate Quarries. Owned by the Maid Marion Locomotive Association, this engine ran at Bressingham Steam Museum in Norfolk until 1971, when she was transferred to the Llanberis Lake Railway. In March 1975 a further transfer brought her to Llanuwchllyn. Her duties are shared by sister engine 'Holy War', withdrawn from Dinorwic in November 1967 and the last steam locomotive to work in a British slate quarry. Part of a third Hunslet 0–4–0ST from Dinorwic can be seen at Llanuwchllyn. Named 'Alice', this locomotive will eventually be rebuilt as an 0–4–2 tender engine.

WELSHPOOL & LLANFAIR LIGHT RAILWAY

HQ and Location	Llanfair Caereinion Station, Llanfair Caereinion, Powys. Llanfair Caereinion Station is immediately alongside the A458 Welshpool–Dolgellau road. Welshpool 9 miles. Nearest BR station: Welshpool; then by Crosville bus.
Track Route	Llanfair Caereinion–Sylfaen (5½ miles; 8½ miles with the Welshpool extension). Gauge: 2 ft 6 in.
Times of Opening	Daily from mid-June to mid-September; weekends in April, May and from mid-September to early October; Spring and Autumn Bank Holidays.
Further Information from	The Welshpool and Llanfair Light Railway, The Station, Llanfair Caereinion, Welshpool, Powys, SY21 0SF. Tel: Llanfair Caereinion (0938-82) 441.

The original W & L opened under a Light Railway Order in 1903, and was successively operated by the Cambrian Railway, the Great Western and British Railways. The line connected with the main-line station in Welshpool, and although passenger services ceased in 1931 the railway continued to carry general agricultural traffic until its closure in 1956.

There were many who wished to save the Welshpool and Llanfair, and a preservation society was formed on the pattern of those successfully operating the Talyllyn and Festiniog Railways. The Welshpool and Llanfair Light Railway Preservation Company began work in 1960, and by 1963 the section of line between Llanfair Caereinion and Castle Caereinion was officially reopened to passenger traffic after a lapse of thirty-two years. In 1972 the line was extended to its present terminus at Sylfaen. The company intend to reopen the line as far as Welshpool in the near future, and a new terminus suitable for tourist traffic is being built at Raven Square.

The original engines were 0–6–0Ts No. 1 'The Earl' and No. 2 'The Countess', built for the line in 1902 by Beyer Peacock. These engines served the line unaided until closure in 1956, and after the 1963 reopening they continued to operate all trains for several years.

From the late 1960s onwards the atmosphere of this conservative little line changed as items of stock were gathered in from such diverse places as Europe, West Africa and the West Indies.

The first engine to arrive from abroad was No. 10 'Sir Drefaldwyn', an 0–8–0T built in France by Franco-Belge as one of a once numerous class used by the German Military Field Railways during World War II. After the war this engine went to Austria, until transferred to the W & L in 1969. 'Sir Drefaldwyn' is a hefty engine with a high tractive effort and has proved an excellent performer over the line's heavy grades.

Two years later No. 12, 'Joan', arrived from the West Indies. This engine was built by Kerr Stuart of Stoke-on-Trent in 1927 and spent most of her working life hauling train-loads of sugar cane on the tropical island of Antigua. Equally notable is No. 14, a 2–6–2T built by Hunslet in 1954 as one of a batch of thirty-two similar engines supplied to the Sierra Leone Railways. Rescued in the nick of time, she was shipped back from West Africa in 1975.

Two unique locomotives can be seen from British industrial establishments. The first is No. 6, 'Monarch', a Bagnall 0–4–4–0 articulated four-cylinder simple built in 1953 for Bowater Lloyds Paper Mill at Sittingbourne, Kent. 'Monarch' is extremely large and is the most powerful engine on the W & L. She weighs $28\frac{1}{2}$ tons, has a tractive effort of 12,750 lbs and is distinctive in having an eight-element superheater. In complete contrast comes the diminutive 'Dougal', an 0–4–0T built in 1946 by Andrew Barclay of Kilmarnock for the extensive railway network at Provan Gasworks in Glasgow. 'Dougal' was specially designed for working in confined spaces, and her appearance is most unusual. She is often found on yard shunting duties at Llanfair.

The W & L's coaching stock is culled from many sources, and ex-Admiralty bogies work alongside end-balcony four-wheelers from the Zillertalbahn—a 760 mm line in the Austrian Tyrol. Other overseas stock includes four modern vacuum-fitted main-line vehicles from Sierra Leone. These coaches—built in Gloucester in 1961—were presented to the Sierra Leone Railways to mark the colony's independence.

Thus, while retaining its Edwardian charm, the W&L offers a splendid diversity of interests, from three continents.

FAIRBOURNE RAILWAY

HQ and Location	Beach Road, Fairbourne, Gwynedd. Fairbourne is served by the A493 Dolgellau–Tywyn road. Fairbourne BR station is immediately alongside the Fairbourne Railway station.
Track Route	Fairbourne Terminus–Barmouth Ferry ($2\frac{1}{4}$ miles). Gauge: 15 in.
Times of Opening	Daily over Easter week; then Sundays until Spring Bank Holiday; then daily until mid-October.

Further Information from   The Manager, Fairbourne Railway Ltd, Beach Road, Fairbourne, Gwynedd, LL38 2EX. Tel: Fairbourne 362; Bontddu 237.

As a result of Fairbourne's expansion during the late 19th century, a 2 ft gauge horse-drawn tramway was built for carrying freight and passengers from the village to Penrhyn Point, where they connected with the ferry across the Mawddach Estuary to Barmouth.

In 1916 the track was converted to a width of 15 in. by Narrow Gauge Railways Ltd—a subsidiary of Bassett Lowke—and steam traction was introduced. The railway closed during World War II and was severely damaged by the weather and military operations. Despite fears that it would never reopen a company acquired the railway, and it was entirely reopened from 1947 onwards.

Fairbourne remains today an idyllic seaside resort. The line starts in the village centre and runs through sand dunes alongside the open sea. Three station halts are incorporated and passengers have marvellous views of the spectacular countryside (especially when riding in the line's open coaches). A picnic site is provided at Barmouth terminus. During inclement weather the service may be restricted or cancelled, but a flag flown at Barmouth Ferry terminus indicates when the trains are running.

Four steam locomotives are allocated to the railway, the oldest being a Bassett Lowke Atlantic named 'Count Louis'. Atlantics have long been but a memory, and this engine is a refreshing reminder of a bygone period of steam design. She is typically English in appearance, being based on Ivatt's larger Great Northern Atlantics. She came from the estate of the Polish Count Louis Zborowski, the famous racing driver and miniature railway enthusiast. The logical development of the 'Atlantic' was the 'Pacific', and Fairbourne's Guest-Twining 'Ernest W. Twining' in Caledonian blue livery ably demonstrates this later phase of steam's evolution. The final two engines are 2–4–2s named 'Katie' and 'Sian' built by Guest of Stourbridge in 1954 and 1963 respectively. They were specially designed with outside frames and enclosed bearings to prevent sand blowing into the engine's moving parts.

Occasionally, some of Fairbourne's engines work a season on other famous 15 in. gauge lines, such as the Romney Hythe and

141

Dymchurch and the Ravenglass and Eskdale. During 1976 'Count Louis' spent a whole season delighting visitors at Ravenglass, while 'Sian' arrived later that year to take part in the R&E's centenary celebrations.

TALYLLYN RAILWAY

HQ and Location	Wharf Station, Tywyn, Gwynedd. Tywyn is situated on the A493 road some 16 miles west of Machynlleth. Nearest BR station: Tywyn (easy access to Wharf Station).
Track Route	Tywyn Wharf–Nant Gwernol (7¼ miles). Gauge: 2 ft 3 in.
Times of Opening	Daily from end of March to end of September; daily during October except Mondays and Fridays.
Further Information from	Talyllyn Railway Co., Wharf Station, Tywyn, Gwynedd, LL36 9EY. Tel: Tywyn (0654) 710472.

The Talyllyn Railway was opened in 1866 to carry slate from Bryneglwys to Tywyn. A combination of horse power and cable-worked inclines was used as far as Nant Gwernol after which steam locomotives took over. Passenger services commenced on the line the following year. Closure seemed imminent in 1910 when the operators abandoned their lease of the slate quarry, but the line was saved by Henry Haydn Jones, Liberal MP for Merioneth, who bought the quarry and railway. The quarry finally closed in 1947, but the railway continued until Sir Henry's death in 1951. The railway was in an advanced state of decay and closure seemed inevitable. Fortunately the value of the Talyllyn was recognized by a few, and in 1951 the Talyllyn Railway Preservation Society was formed. This action heralded the world's first successful preservation scheme.

After twenty-five years of dedicated work by enthusiasts, the

Talyllyn has been completely revitalized. Volunteer labour for running the railway is drawn from the seven-thousand-strong membership of the Talyllyn Railway Preservation Society, and only a limited number of permanent staff are employed. Until 1976 the line terminated at Abergynolwyn, but today trains run through to the old terminus at Nant Gwernol, situated at the foot of the Alltwyllt Incline. The Talyllyn is Britain's only 2 ft 3 in. gauge railway.

The two original locomotives remain at work, and visitors see them in a beautifully restored condition; both were built by Fletcher Jennings of Whitehaven. No. 1 'Talyllyn' is an 0–4–2ST, and No. 2, 'Dolgoch', an 0–4–0WT; their building dates are 1865 and 1866 respectively.

Four additional engines have been added to the Talyllyn's roster since preservation, and two came from the nearby Corris Railway. These are 'Sir Haydn', an 0–4–2ST built by Hughes of Loughborough in 1878, and 'Edward Thomas', a quite different design of 0–4–2ST from Kerr Stuart of Stoke-on-Trent in 1921. The other two engines are 'Douglas' and 'Irish Pete'. The former—an Andrew Barclay 0–4–0WT of 1918—was presented by the RAF

Talyllyn Railway No. 6 'Douglas', an Andrew Barclay 0–4–0 Well Tank of 1918, leaves Dolgoch with an up-train.

in 1953; the latter was built by Barclay's as a 3 ft gauge 0–4–0WT for the Irish Turf Board. This engine has been completely rebuilt at Tywyn as a 2 ft 3 in. gauge 0–4–2T.

The Talyllyn's original coaches have been supplemented by historic examples from the Corris Railway and Glyn Valley Tramway. More recently eight new bogie coaches, built in a period style, have also been added.

The line climbs inland from the coast and passes through majestic scenery with fine views of Cader Idris. Many interesting birds are likely to be seen during the journey, and Bird Rock—a celebrated inland nesting site for cormorant and shag—can be reached by a scenic walk from Dolgoch. From Abergynolwyn passengers can take a bus to Talyllyn Lake. The train concludes its journey to Nant Gwernol by threading a shelf cut into the mountainside, the terminus being located on the edge of an enormous ravine. Here passengers can either pause to enjoy the spectacular views or walk to the old slate workings. These are very dangerous and great care must be exercised when exploring them.

The fabulous Narrow Gauge Railway Museum adjoins the platform at Tywyn Wharf Station. This museum was opened in 1956 and has been continually extended in scope. Eight locomotives are present, and the collection includes equipment from narrow-gauge railways all over Britain. This museum has considerable educational value and is a popular destination for school parties. The collection is operated by the Narrow Gauge Railway Museum Trust.

VALE OF RHEIDOL RAILWAY

HQ and Location	Aberystwyth Station, Aberystwyth, Dyfed. Aberystwyth is situated on the main A487 Welsh Coast road. Vale of Rheidol trains depart from Aberystwyth BR station.

Track Route	Aberystwyth–Devil's Bridge (11¾ miles). Gauge: 1 ft 11½ in.
Times of Opening	Daily from late March to early October.
Further Information from	Vale of Rheidol Railway, Aberystwyth Station, Aberystwyth, Dyfed. Tel: Aberystwyth 612377; or Room 3, Divisional Manager's Office, British Rail, Station Road, Stoke-on-Trent, Staffordshire, ST4 2AA.

When steam locomotives finally disappeared from the main lines during August 1968, there remained three narrow-gauge engines hard at work on a remote line in Central Wales. Known as the Vale of Rheidol this railway remains under BR ownership and is exclusively steam-worked. The line is aided by the voluntary Vale of Rheidol Railway Supporters Association.

The Vale of Rheidol Railway opened in 1902 for goods and passenger traffic, and was absorbed into the Cambrian Railways in 1913.

hree steam locomotives still operate on British Rail, on the line from Aberystwyth to Devil's ridge. Here is No. 8 'Llywelyn', built at Swindon in 1923.

After the grouping, the V of R became a part of the Great Western, and under the nationalization of railways in 1948 it passed into the Western Region of British Railways. Today the V of R forms part of the London Midland Region of British Rail.

As the line climbs inland from the coast it passes through the spectacular mountain scenery of the Rheidol Valley, and when Devil's Bridge station is reached the trains are 680 ft above sea level. The Devil's Bridge itself is a tripartite structure of which the lowest section is mediaeval in origin. The bridge is three minutes' walk from the station. Another wonderful sight at Devil's Bridge is the 400 ft Mynach Waterfalls—best viewed from the bottom of the steps which lead into the gorge.

The line is worked by three specially designed 2–6–2Ts. Numbers 7 and 8, 'Owain Glyndwr' and 'Llywelyn', were built at Swindon in 1923; No. 9, 'Prince of Wales', was one of two built by Davies and Metcalfe of Romiley in 1902 for the line's opening. The other engine 'Edward VII' was withdrawn in 1932, presumably because winter passenger services ceased the previous year. These two engines were the only ones ever built by Davies & Metcalfe.

The line has open coaching stock built to a 1923 GWR design, along with some fully enclosed vehicles of 1938 with steel underframes and steel-panelled sides. Engines and stock are painted in standard BR livery, complete with white insignia. Trains comprise six coaches and a brake-van, and take one hour to reach Devil's Bridge.

GWILI RAILWAY

HQ and Location   Bronwydd Arms Station, Dyfed. Bronwydd Arms Station is situated 2 miles north of Carmarthen on the A484 Newcastle Emlyn road. Nearest BR station: Carmarthen;

	Crosville buses connect with Gwili Railway. (No buses run on Sundays.)
Track Route	Northwards from Bronwydd Arms Station ($1\frac{1}{4}$ miles). Gauge: Standard.
Times of Opening	Weekends and Bank Holidays during the summer season.
Further Information from	Gwili Railway, Bronwydd Arms Station, Dyfed; or registered office: Gwili Railway, Great West Chambers, Angel Street, Neath, West Glamorgan, SAII IRS.

The Gwili Railway Company are reopening a part of the former Great Western line from Carmarthen to Aberystwyth, and a deposit has been paid to British Rail for the eight miles of trackbed from Abergwili Junction—immediately north of Carmarthen—to Llanpumpsaint. The initial one-and-a-quarter-mile section was opened for steam services during 1978.

The first trains were worked by the company's Peckett 0–4–0ST 'Merlin', which had been specially overhauled at Ironrails Yard, Carmarthen, and during 1978 another Peckett 0–4–0ST was being restored there for eventual use on the line. By far the oldest engine present is Manning Wardle 0–6–0ST 'Aldwyth', built in 1882.

The Gwili Railway Company draw voluntary support from the Gwili Railway Preservation Society.

Area 7. North-West

EAST LANCASHIRE RAILWAY PRESERVATION SOCIETY

HQ and Location Bury Transport Museum, Castlecroft Road, Bury, Lancs. Bury is situated on the A56 road 8 miles north of Manchester. The museum is a few minutes walk from Bury BR station.

Gauge Standard.

Times of Opening Saturdays and Sundays; Easter Monday, Spring and Late Summer Bank Holidays. Steaming on last Sunday of each month from March to September, and during the Bank Holidays.

Further Information from East Lancashire Railway Preservation Society, Bury Transport Museum, Castlecroft Road, Bury, Lancashire, BL9 0LN. Tel: 061 764 7790.

The East Lancashire Railway Preservation Society aim to operate a steam service over the old East Lancashire Railway's line between Bury and Rawtenstall. A quarter-mile length of track has already been laid, and brake-van rides take place on steaming days. The East Lancashire Railway was a constituent of the Lancashire and Yorkshire Railway and had a works at Bury.

Society members have converted the former East Lancashire Railway goods depot at Bury into a transport museum. In addition to the steam locomotives and rolling stock the visitor can see an

Carlisle

Penrith

Whitehaven

*Ravenglass &
Eskdale Rly* Boot
Dalegarth

Ravenglass

Lakeside
Haverthwaite *Lakeside &
Haverthwaite
Rly*

Isle of Man

Douglas
Isle of Man Rly
Port Erin

Barrow
Ulverston
Carnforth

*Steamtown
Rly Museum*

Lancaster

Blackpool
Lytham *Lytham Creek Rly*
Preston

Southport *Steamport*

*East Lancashire Rly
Preservation Society* Bury

Manchester

Liverpool

Crewe

AREA 7

NORTH-WEST

CUMBRIA   LANCASHIRE   CHESHIRE
ISLE OF MAN   MERSEYSIDE

interesting collection of cars and buses, a steamroller and a fire engine. A working model railway is also incorporated into the site.

The steam locomotives are all of industrial design and include two handsome Hudswell Clarke 0–6–0Ts once owned by the Manchester Ship Canal Company. There are a couple of Andrew Barclay 0–4–0STs, the oldest being a veteran of 1904 from the Yates Duxbury Paper Works at Bury, the other from Burnley Gas Works. Another Yates Duxbury engine in the museum is 'Annie', a Peckett 0–4–0ST, and the largest and most modern engine is a hefty Robert Stephenson and Hawthorn 0–6–0T built in 1951. This engine came from Meaford Power Station in Staffordshire.

STEAMPORT

HQ and Location	Steamport, Derby Road Motive Power Depot, Southport, Merseyside. Southport is situated on the A565, 20 miles north of Liverpool. Nearest BR station: Southport Chapel Street.
Gauge	Standard.
Times of Opening	Daily from Spring Bank Holiday to mid-September. (At least one engine in steam every Sunday.) Weekend afternoons from mid-September to Spring Bank Holiday. (At least one engine in steam on the last Sunday in the month.)
Further Information from	The Publicity Officer, Steamport Southport Ltd, Derby Road, Southport, Merseyside, PR9 0TY. Tel: Southport 30693.

This lively museum is centered upon the old Lancashire and Yorkshire Railway's steam shed at Southport. The depot, abandoned by BR in 1966, was leased in 1973 to the Southport Locomotive

Transport Museum Society, whose intention was to use the site as a working exhibition centre of transport relics. The society faced a formidable task: the depot had been heavily vandalized, no track remained and water and electricity had been disconnected.

The entire depot site was gradually returned to life; track was found in old industrial sidings, and the first exhibits began to arrive. Steamport was opened to the public in 1974 and has now become Merseyside's Railway and Transport Museum. In addition to the steam locomotives, buses, fire engines, trams, steamrollers, a model railway and a museum of small exhibits can be seen.

Engines include LMS 'Black 5' No. 44806 'Magpie' and BR Standard 4 2–6–0 No. 76079, rescued from the Barry scrapyard by a group of enthusiasts who formed a company called Frogstone Ltd. Another ex-main-liner is LMS 'Jinty' No. 47298, belonging to the Liverpool Locomotive Preservation Group—who also own the centre's Avonside 0–6–0ST 'Lucy' and Barclay 0–4–0ST 'Efficient'.

Altogether ten steam locomotives can be seen in the authentic

Brake-van rides around Southport Transport Museum's yards are ably undertaken by this North Western Gas Board Peckett 0–4–0ST, built in 1941.

atmosphere of the longhouse, and brake-van rides are given around the yard on steaming days. The society's aim is to bridge the half-mile to Southport Central Station.

LYTHAM MOTIVE POWER MUSEUM AND LYTHAM CREEK RAILWAY

HQ and Location	Lytham Motive Power Museum, Lytham Industrial Estate, Lytham, Lancs. Lytham is situated on the A584 road 8 miles south of Blackpool. Preston 12 miles. Nearest BR station: Lytham.
Track Route	Lytham Creek Railway runs through the motive power museum ($\frac{1}{3}$ mile). Steam working on Sundays. Gauge: 1 ft 10$\frac{3}{4}$ in.
Times of Opening	Daily from mid-May to mid-October, except Mondays and Fridays.
Further Information from	James Morris, Helical Springs Ltd, Dock Road, Lytham, Lancs. Tel: Lytham 733122.

The standard-gauge engines in this collection are static exhibits, but on Sundays the narrow-gauge Lytham Creek Railway operates with an 0–4–0ST named 'Jonathan', built by Hunslet in 1898. Before arriving at Lytham, this engine spent her entire working life at the Dinorwic slate quarries in Caernarvonshire.

The standard-gauge engines form an imposing collection: all are of the 0–4–0 type and many are imaginatively painted in well-known pre-grouping liveries. Especially rare is the ex-North British Railway 'Pug' built in 1887 to an 1882 design by Matthew Holmes. This diminutive engine shunted Leith Docks for many years and became LNER 'Y9' Class No. 68095. She was finally withdrawn from St Margarets shed, Edinburgh, in 1962. Equally rare is a Neilson Crane Tank named 'Snipey' built in 1890 for the Hodbarrow Mining Company at Millom. This engine was transferred to Lytham in 1968 and is now decked in North Eastern colours. Another industrial antique is 'Vulcan'—a former works shunter at the Vulcan Foundry, Newton-le-Willows.

Other engines include a Hawthorn Leslie in LBSCR livery, a Hudswell Clarke in LNWR 'Greater Britain' Diamond Jubilee Scarlet; and a Peckett in L&Y livery. The most modern engine is 'Susan', a 1951-built vertical-boiler 'Sentinel' which formerly hailed from the Chesterfield Tube Company. Many smaller exhibits of railway interest can be seen, such as the 6 ft-diameter driving wheels of Stanier 'Black 5' No. 45140, and a vintage model railway.

Visitors will also see exhibits relating to road engines, cars and aircraft, including a 1902 Burnell single-crank compound engine, a 1933 Austin saloon car, the propellers from a Britannia aircraft and the cockpit of a Spitfire. Two operational aircraft are also on display: a Provost and a T11 Vampire.

STEAMTOWN RAILWAY MUSEUM

HQ and Location	Steamtown Railway Museum, Warton Road, Carnforth, Lancashire. Carnforth is situated on the A6 between Lancaster and Kendal; also easily reached from Inter-section 35 on the M6 Motorway. Lancaster 6 miles. Nearest BR station: Carnforth (museum a few minutes' walk from the station).
Gauge	Standard.
Times of Opening	Daily throughout the year (except Christmas Day). Steam days: Sundays from March to October; Saturdays from May to September; daily from mid-July to end of August.

Further Information from

Steamtown Railway Museum Ltd, Warton Road, Carnforth, Lancs. Tel: Carnforth 2625 and 4220.

Steamtown is one of Britain's foremost railway preservation centres with some thirty locomotives. The centre is a fully authentic locomotive shed and yard which, until 1969, was operated as British Rail's 10A Carnforth depot. It was one of the last sheds in Britain to retain steam locomotives and had an active allocation until 1968. In 1967 a group of enthusiasts formed a company to take over the shed from BR. Incorporated into the museum are the shed ashpits, a 75,000-gallon water tower, a 70 ft vacuum turntable, a Midland Railway signal box and a full-sized concrete coaling tower with a holding capacity of 150 tons—the only surviving example of its kind in the world. The twenty-three-acre site has three miles of track, including a mile-long running line for passenger rides and locomotive demonstrations.

Steamtown also serves as a working depot for engines undertaking BR railtours on the approved route between Sellafield, Barrow, Carnforth, Skipton, Leeds, Harrogate, York and Scarborough. The centre also has an arrangement to operate engines from the National Railway Museum at York.

The Crane Locomotive was an offshoot from the mainstream of steam locomotive development. This is 'Glenfield', built by Andrew Barclay in 1902 and now at Steamtown Carnforth.

Five famous Pacifics, drawn from the best in British and Continental practice, can be seen at Steamtown. These are ex-LNER A3 'Flying Scotsman', A4 'Sir Nigel Gresley' and Southern Merchant Navy 'Canadian Pacific'. France is represented by a four-cylinder 231K, originally built in 1914 for the PLM and subsequently rebuilt by Chapelon. This engine was often employed on the Golden Arrow between Calais and Paris until 1969. In marked contrast is German 012 104–6, a standard three-cylinder engine which was streamlined when built in 1940.

Among the 4–6–0s present are three LMS Stanier 'Black 5's and the considerably larger No. 850 'Lord Nelson', introduced by Maunsell in 1926 for the Southern Railway's heavy boat trains. The sole surviving Gresley three-cylinder 2–6–2 'Green Arrow' can also be seen. These engines were introduced in 1936 for working fast freights over the east coast main line.

Two fundamental 19th century types are represented also: 'Hardwick', a LNER Webb 2–4–0 express passenger engine of 1878, and No. 1122, a classically proportioned inside-cylinder 0–6–0 goods engine built for the Lancashire and Yorkshire Railway in 1892 to an 1889 design by Aspinall. Smaller main-line engines in Steamtown's collection include Ivatt 2–6–0 No. 6441 in red livery; GW 0–6–2T No. 5643, and a German Deutsche Reichsbahn Class '80' 0–6–0T. The ten industrial engines are extremely varied and include a Fireless, an 0–4–0 Crane Tank and a Sentinel named 'Gasbag'.

Steamtown's authentic atmosphere is heightened by an operational model railway based on Berkhamsted in the LNWR, LMS and BR eras. The layout has 50 locomotives, 100 coaches and 200 wagons.

LAKESIDE & HAVERTHWAITE RAILWAY

HQ and Location   Haverthwaite Station, Nr Newby
                             Bridge, Ulverston, Lancashire.

155

Haverthwaite is situated on the A590 trunk road 15 miles north-east of Barrow-in-Furness. Nearest BR station Ulverston.

Track Route Lakeside–Haverthwaite ($3\frac{1}{2}$ miles). Gauge: Standard.

Times of Opening Daily from mid-May to end of October.

Further Information from The Lakeside & Haverthwaite Railway Co. Ltd, Haverthwaite Station, Nr Newby Bridge, Ulverston, Lancs. Tel: 04483 594.

In 1869 the Furness Railway opened an eight-mile branch line from Lakeside on the shore of Windermere to Plumpton Junction on the Carnforth–Barrow-in-Furness mainline. This enabled trains to connect with the steamers on Lake Windermere and attracted a thriving tourist traffic. Inevitably this traffic was seasonal, and by 1965 the line was regarded as uneconomic and passenger services were withdrawn under the Beeching programme. A few freight trains continued to service Backbarrow Furnaces near Haverthwaite, but upon closure of the foundry in 1967 the line was abandoned completely.

A private company was immediately formed to purchase the line and reinstate services, but their whole objective could not be achieved, and they were forced to concentrate upon the section between Haverthwaite and Lakeside. After three years of negotiation with British Rail, this part of the line was reopened in 1973 by the late Eric Treacy, Bishop of Wakefield. Today the line is operated by the Lakeside and Haverthwaite Railway Company and supported by the Lakeside Railway Society on a volunteer basis.

The line follows the beautiful River Leven Valley and has an intermediate station at Newby Bridge Halt. This station had been closed during the 1930s and was restored as a special project by the Blackpool branch of the Lakeside Railway Society.

Two ex-LMS Fairburn 2–6–4Ts, nos. 2073 and 2085, arrived on the line in 1970. These engines are the only preserved examples of their kind and they are ideal for the Lakeside branch. This class was once found on medium-distance passenger services throughout the old LMS system, and 277 examples were built between 1945

156

and 1951. No. 2073 is finished in LNWR Blackberry Black and No. 2085 in Caledonian Blue.

The two Fairburns are supplemented by Nos. 5 and 6, a couple of delightful Hudswell Clarke 0–6–0STs built for the Appleby-Frodingham Steel Company. No. 6 was the original engine supplied in 1919, and her success led to many others being built.

Visitors will also see an attractive Bagnall 0–6–0ST named 'Princess'. This engine was transferred to Lakeside from the Lytham Motive Power Museum and was originally one of a batch of identical engines which worked in Preston Docks. Another Preston engine is the little Peckett 0–4–0ST 'Caliban' purchased by two society members in 1967 from Cortauld.

Lakeside's motive power roster is completed by a couple of Austerities. One is a Giesl chimneyed workhorse named 'Repulse' from the National Coal Board; the other is the ever-popular red-liveried 'Cumbria', purchased from the Ministry of Defence Weapon Testing Depot at Shoeburyness in Essex.

RAVENGLASS AND ESKDALE RAILWAY

HQ and Location	Ravenglass Station, Ravenglass, Cumbria. Ravenglass is situated on the A595 Barrow–Whitehaven road. The Ravenglass and Eskdale line adjoins BR Ravenglass station.
Track Route	Ravenglass–Dalegarth (7 miles). Gauge: 15 in.
Times of Opening	Daily from end of March to end of October; limited winter service from 30 October.
Further Information from	The Ravenglass and Eskdale Railway Co. Ltd, Ravenglass, Cumbria, CA18 1SW. Tel: Ravenglass (06577) 226.

Known as 'L'al Ratty', this scenic narrow-gauge line begins at Ravenglass on the Irish Sea coast and climbs through two beautiful

Lakeland valleys to Dalegarth. Up to Irton Road station, the line follows the Rivert Irt and is dramatically overshadowed by Muncaster Fell—a haven for buzzards. On entering the Esk Valley a 1-in-36 gradient is encountered before reaching Dalegarth, where a picnic area is located beside the river. One journey takes 40 minutes, and during the peak season ten trains run each way daily.

The Ravenglass and Eskdale was opened in 1876 to carry iron ore from the mines at Boot to the Furness Railway's main line at Ravenglass. In those early days the gauge was 3 ft. The mines failed in 1882 and, after years of difficulties, the railway was closed in 1913. It lay derelict for two years until Narrow Gauge Railways Ltd reinstated it as a tourist attraction and converted the gauge to 15 in. Additional good fortune came in 1922 with the opening of a quarry at Beckfoot, but it closed in 1953. During the years 1958–9 the railway was offered for sale, without success, and by 1960 closure was threatened. A preservation society was formed, and with the aid of Colin Gilbert—a Birmingham stockbroker—the line was saved. It remains commercially operated today but is actively supported by the preservation society.

The engines burn coke to avoid smuts showering over passengers in the open coaches. The newest engine owned by the Ravenglass and Eskdale Company is a 2–6–2 named 'Northern Rock'. She was built in 1976 and is finished in Muscat livery. Also active is a Heywood 0–8–2 of 1894 named 'River Irt' and a Davey Paxman 2–8–2 of 1923 named 'River Esk'. The other popular engine is 'River Mite', a 2–8–2 owned by the preservation society. This engine—which incorporated an old frame and new boiler—was assembled by Clarkson of York in 1966 and was transported across the Pennines to Ravenglass on a trailer hauled by the traction engine 'Providence'.

ISLE OF MAN RAILWAY

HQ and Location   Douglas Station, Douglas, Isle of Man. Douglas is situated on the west coast of the island. The island is reached by air from Liverpool to Castletown, or by sea direct to Douglas. Respective journey times: 35 minutes and 4 hours.

Track Route   Douglas–Port Erin (15½ miles). Gauge: 3 ft.

Times of Opening   Daily from mid-May to late September (Saturdays excluded).

Further Information from   Isle of Man Railways, Terminus Building, Strathallan Crescent, Douglas, Isle of Man. Tel: Douglas (0624) 4549 and 4540.

The Isle of Man Railway operates some of the most aesthetically pleasing steam engines in the world. All are vintage Beyer Peacock 2–4–0Ts which were first introduced in 1873. The oldest active example in the ten-engine fleet is 'Loch', built in 1874, and the most recent is 'Kissack' of 1910. These engines resemble a smaller version of Beyer Peacock's celebrated standard-gauge 4–4–0Ts built for the Metropolitan Inner Circle from 1864.

The Isle of Man Railway is one of the most colourful vintage railways in the world. Here is 'Loch'—a Beyer Peacock 2–4–0T built in 1874.

During the 1870s, a fine railway network was developed throughout the island, beginning with the Isle of Man Railway Company's line from Douglas to Peel in 1873; this was followed by the south line to Port Erin one year later. The company intended to include Ramsey in the system, but no funds remained. Ramsey's inhabitants funded their own line, the Manx Northern, which connected with the Douglas–Peel route in 1879. The Manx Northern was absorbed by the larger company in 1904.

The entire network was closed during 1965 despite widespread protest, and in 1967 the system was leased to the Marquess of Ailsa, who intended to restore it for tourist traffic. A grand reopening took place that year, but the lines to Peel and Ramsey were closed again in 1968 and have since been lifted. Today only the south line to Port Erin survives and is operated by the Isle of Man Railway Company with financial guarantees from Manx Tynwald, and vigorous assistance from the Isle of Man Railway Society.

Douglas station is a red-bricked edifice of imposing Victorian proportions. It has a brooding atmosphere of better days gone by and includes a huge booking hall and four covered platforms. The

'Hutchinson' and 'Maitland'—both Beyer Peacock 2–4–0Ts—pictured leaving Douglas simultaneously during the Isle of Man Railway's reopening celebration in 1968.

journey to Port Erin is similar to that made by rail travellers a century ago—especially when the 105-year-old 'Loch' heads the train.

Southbound trains face a two-and-a-half-mile climb to the cliff tops above Port Soderick, famous in Victorian times for its smugglers' caves. As the train coasts downwards towards Ballasalla a magnificent ocean vista opens up, and St Michael's island can clearly be seen. Next comes Castletown, once the island's capital and the largest town on the line. From here the railway heads across the plains and passes through lush meadows between foothills and the sea. Port St Mary is noted for sandy beaches, and the cliffs between here and Port Erin are spectacular.

The railway museum at Port Erin includes locomotives, stock and many small exhibits. The island's first engine, 'Sutherland' of 1873, is on display, along with the larger 'Mannin', built in 1926 and the last engine to arrive on the island. Other railway attractions offered by the Isle of Man are the Manx Electric Railway and the Snaefell Mountain Railway.

Area 8. North-East

MIDDLETON RAILWAY

HQ and Location

Tunstall Road, Leeds 11. Access from the M1 Motorway (Exit 45). Nearest BR station: Leeds City; then by bus (routes 74 or 76) from the station.

Track Route

Tunstall Road–Middleton (Park Gates) ($1\frac{1}{4}$ miles). Gauge: Standard.

Times of Opening

Trains run every weekend afternoon from Easter to end of October; Bank Holidays between these dates.

Further Information from

Middleton Railway, Garnet Road, Leeds, LS11 5JY. Tel: Leeds 645424.

The Middleton Colliery Railway was built in 1758 to convey coal in horse-drawn wagons from the pits at Belle Isle and Middleton to Leeds. The high cost of horse feed encouraged the owners to consider alternative forms of haulage, and in 1812 the line received the world's first commercially successful steam locomotives. These engines were built by Matthew Murray of Leeds using John Blenkinsop's rack and pinion system for adhesion, and on 12 August 1812 crowds watched a public demonstration of a $5\frac{1}{2}$-ton locomotive pulling a 26-ton train at 5 mph. George Stephenson also came to see the engines at work.

Named 'Salamanca' and 'Prince Regent', these two engines were later joined by a futher pair and remained in service until 1835. The railway carried coal to Leeds until 1947, when the line was

AREA 8

NORTH-EAST

YORKSHIRE DURHAM NORTHUMBERLAND
CLEVELAND TYNE & WEAR
NORTH HUMBERSIDE

Berwick upon Tweed

Newcastle upon Tyne

Sunniside
Marley Stanley
Tanfield Rly Hill
Bowes Bridge

*North of
England Open
Air Museum*

Chester-le-Street

Durham

Darlington

Whitby

Grosmont

North Yorkshire Moors Rly

Thirsk

Pickering

Scarborough

Yorkshire Dales Rly
Embsay
Skipton

Harrogate

York Layerthorpe
National   Derwent Valley Rly
Rly Museum   Dunnington

Keighley
*Keighley & Worth
Valley Rly*
Haworth   Leeds
Bradford *Middleton Rly*
Oxenhope

Hull

Sheffield

cut back to Hunslet Moor, and in 1960 was threatened with complete closure. A preservation scheme was started, and two centuries after the line's inception it became the first standard-gauge railway to be preserved by amateurs.

Passengers ride the system, in open goods wagons or an ex-LMS brake-van. Trains run every half hour, and the present route includes a 1-in-27 gradient and a tunnel under the M1 motorway. Eight steam locomotives are present, all of the industrial type except No. 1310—an ex-North Eastern Railway 'Y7' 0–4–0ST built in 1891—and an ex-Danish State Railway 0–4–0WT of 1893. Both engines belong to the Steam Power Trust. Other engines include a rare Borrows 0–4–0WT named 'Windle', built in 1909 to an 1866 design and presented to the Middleton Railway Trust by Pilkington Bros in 1961. Borrows of St Helens were noted for their four-coupled well tanks and around forty examples were built. A vertical-boiler Sentinel can also be seen. The Middleton's collection embraces side tanks, well tanks, saddle tanks and vertical-boiler engines all of the 0–4–0 type, and a hundred-year-old steam crane is employed on track maintenance duties.

At present engines not in use are stored in private factory premises on Garnet Road, and admission is generally limited to members and parties of visitors; but the trust hopes to have its own locomotive shed in the near future. The Middleton is a registered charity, and all work is carried out by volunteers.

KEIGHLEY AND WORTH VALLEY RAILWAY

HQ and Location	Haworth Station, Haworth, Keighley, West Yorkshire. Haworth is situated 9 miles west of Bradford. KWVR trains run into Keighley BR station (on the Leeds–Carlisle main line).
Track Route	Keighley–Oxenhope (5 miles). Gauge: Standard.

Times of Opening	Trains run every weekend and Bank Holiday; daily during July and August.
Further Information from	Keighley and Worth Valley Railway Ltd, Haworth Station, Haworth, Keighley, West Yorks, BD22 8NJ. Tel: Haworth (0535) 43629.

The Worth Valley line was opened in 1867 as a branch of the Midland Railway from Keighley up to Oxenhope. It was closed by BR in 1962, and simultaneously the Keighley and Worth Valley Railway Preservation Society was formed. The reopening occurred on 29 June 1968—101 years after the line's inception.

During the five-mile journey to Oxenhope the trains climb to 330 ft on an average gradient of 1–in–76, with a maximum section of 1–in–58. The Worth Valley trains leave Keighley from the British Rail station and, having passed through Ingrow, arrive at Damens—for years regarded as the smallest 'full-sized' station in Britain. Through rolling West Riding countryside, with stone cottages perched on the hillsides, the line continues to Oakworth, widely known as the principal location for the filming of 'The Railway Children'. Having passed through Mytholmes tunnel, the trains run into Haworth, the home of the Brontë sisters. The Worth Valley's locomotive running shed and workshops are situated here. After a further mile through open country the rural terminus of Oxenhope is reached. Most passengers visit the fine exhibition shed, containing a wide variety of locomotives, before returning down the valley.

Over thirty steam engines grace the Worth Valley. Particularly interesting is the range of five classes built for Army service during World War II. These classes are the Stanier '8F' 2–8–0 along with their Austerity counterpart the Riddles 'W.D.' 2–8–0; the American 'S160' 2–8–0; the Hunslet Austerity 0–6–0ST and the United States Army Transportation Corps (USATC) 0–6–0T.

The Stanier 8Fs are represented by No. 8431, rescued from the Barry scrapyard, while Austerity 2–8–0 No. 1931 was miraculously returned to Britain from the Swedish State Railways. The S160s were specifically built to the British loading gauge, and the Worth Valley's engine was purchased from the Polish State Railways, upon which the type remains active today. The Hunslet Austerities were initially built in readiness for the Allied Invasion of Europe in 1943, and several engines of this type are active on the Worth Valley. The USATC 0–6–0Ts were their American equivalent and these chunky side tanks saw prolific service throughout Europe. The type is well represented on the Worth Valley by engine No. 72 which ended her days in BR service as the shed pilot at Guildford.

Many Worth Valley engines hail from the former LMS fold and these include Stanier 'Black 5' 5212 and 'Crab' No. 42765, saved from Barry scrapyard. Ivatt 2–6–2T No. 41241 is a popular engine on passenger trains and looks glorious in her red livery.

From the LMS constituents is '4F' 0–6–0 3924, built in 1920 to a Midland Railway design of 1911. The Lancashire and York-

A brace of Hunslet Austerities storm along the Worth Valley line near Haworth. In the lead is No. 57, ably assisted to the rear by 'Brussels'.

shire Railway is in evidence with veteran Barton Wright 0–6–0 No. 52044 of 1883 along with three engines from the L&Y Saddle Tanks fund—two 0–4–0ST Pugs and 0–6–0ST No. 752, built in 1881 as a standard shunting design.

The Great Western is represented by one of their standard '5700' Class 0–6–0 Pannier Tanks along with a unique Taff Vale Railway 0–6–2T of 1889. Only one Pacific is allocated to the Worth Valley— ex-Southern Railway 34092 'City of Wells' in original air-smoothed condition. Several BR standards are present including Class '4' 2–6–4T 80002, Class '4' 4–6–0 75078 and Class '2' 2–6–0 78022.

The oldest engine is 'Bellerophon', an 0–6–0 Well Tank built by the Haydock Foundry in 1874. Another distinguished veteran is Manning Wardle 0–6–0ST 'Sir Berkeley', which began life as a contractor's engine during the construction of the Manchester Sheffield and Lincolnshire Railway and ended her days on the Northamptonshire ironfield at Byfield in 1964. Rather more modern in appearance are a pair of Hudswell Clarke 0–6–0Ts from the Manchester Ship Canal Railway.

YORKSHIRE DALES RAILWAY

HQ and Location Embsay Station, Embsay, Nr Skipton, Yorkshire. Embsay is situated to the north of the A59 road from Skipton to Harrogate. Skipton 1½ miles. Nearest BR station: Skipton; then by bus (West Yorks routes 75 or 76) to Embsay.

Track Route Eastwards from Embsay towards Bolton Abbey (1¼ miles). Gauge: Standard.

Times of Opening Every weekend plus Bank Holidays; trains run on selected days.

Further Information from Yorkshire Dales Railway Co., Embsay Station, Embsay, Nr Skipton, Yorkshire.

This railway was founded in 1968 and is situated on the edge of the Yorkshire Dales. The company intend to reinstate steam services between Embsay and Bolton Abbey on the former Midland Railway's line from Skipton to Ilkley.

A fine steam centre has been built at Embsay: the station and signal box have been restored fully, and an engine shed, inspection pits and a run-around loop have been incorporated. Some fifteen steam locomotives are to be seen and all are of the industrial type except Stanier '8F' 2–8–0 No. 48151. This engine was withdrawn from BR upon the cessation of steam traction in 1968 and sent to the Barry scrapyard. She was rescued in 1975 and taken to Embsay for restoration to full working order.

Among the industrial engines are six Hunslet 0–6–0STs, covering several designs including a '50550' Class—the immediate forerunner of the Austerities. Three engines came from the neighbouring Leeds Works of Hudswell Clarke—a standard 'Port of London' Class 0–6–0T and two fine looking 0–6–0STs. In contrast is a 1927-built 0–4–0 VBGT Sentinel from British Tar.

The engines most frequently in use are No. 22, a standard 14 in. 0–4–0ST from Andrew Barclay and 'York No. 1', a Yorkshire Engine Company 0–4–0ST built in 1948 and at time of writing the only working engine from this builder in Britain.

Eventually it is hoped to include several gauges of track to display a wide selection of industrial engines. However, a $9\frac{1}{2}$ in. gauge passenger-carrying model railway is installed and runs on summer Sundays, worked by a handsome 2–4–2 tender engine of 1932 named 'King Tut'.

NATIONAL RAILWAY MUSEUM

HQ and Location   Leeman Road, York. Leeman Road is conveniently reached from the city centre and is a short walk from York BR station.

Gauge   Standard.

Times of Opening	Weekdays and Sunday afternoons. Closed on New Year's Day, Good Friday, May Day, Christmas Eve, Christmas Day and Boxing Day. (Please enquire about other days between Christmas and New Year.)
Further Information from	National Railway Museum, Leeman Road, York, YO2 4XJ. Tel: York (0904) 21261.

Britain's National Railway Museum was opened in September 1975. It houses the largest single display of the National Collection of railway locomotives and rolling stock. During its first twelve months the museum received over two million visitors, and the total had risen to four million within two-and-a-half years. The museum is based on the former York North motive power depot and is complete with two turntables around which are placed the major exhibits.

In addition to the many historically significant locomotives and rolling stock on display the museum embraces the wider aspects of railway operation and includes rolling stock, permanent way, signalling and a comprehensive collection of railwayana. The well-equipped workshops undertake the restoration of exhibits of all sizes. The museum maintains in full working order three of the famous engines in the National Collection—'Hardwicke', 'Green Arrow' and 'Evening Star'.

Parties of visitors are advised to get in touch with the Museum Education Service before their visit. This service offers a choice of illustrated talks and demonstrations in the lecture theatre and a children's study coach.

The locomotives present include some beautifully restored examples from various stages in the steam locomotive's evolution. The visitor will see early passenger engines dating from the 1840s, single wheelers, 0–4–2s and 2–4–0s from mid- to late 19th century along with late Victorian period 4–4–0s. Goods engines include 'Agenoria', an 0–4–0 of 1829, a Great Western Railway heavy-duty '28XX' Class 2–8–0 of 1905, and the Class '9F' 2–10–0 92220 'Evening Star', the last steam locomotive built by British Railways and completed as recently as 1960.

Old Furness Railway 0–4–0 No. 3 'Coppernob'—built in 1846—stands on the turntable at th *National Railway Museum.*

The later years of steam development are represented by the superb Stanier Pacific 46229 'Duchess of Hamilton', while another modern express passenger engine—the rebuilt Bulleid Merchant Navy Pacific 35029 'Ellerman Lines'—has been sectioned for detailed inspection. But it is probably the ex-LNER 'A4' 4468 'Mallard' which captures the imagination of most visitors, for on 3 July 1938 this engine attained a world speed record for steam traction of 126 mph.

The two tracks which connect the museum with British Railways enable the exchange of exhibits between the public areas of the museum and the annexe, so that the items actually on display are frequently changed (and all those referred to will not necessarily be on view at any one time).

Exchanges also take place with the various private operating railways. A highlight was the transfer of the pioneer GNR small Atlantic 'Henry Oakley' to the Keighley & Worth Valley Railway, for the summer of 1977. Locomotives and coaches from various societies have also been on display in the Museum. The Friends of the National Railway Museum was set up in 1977 to encourage and foster the work of the museum.

The National Railway Museum does not operate any steam services of its own, but certain locomotives based at York are used for main-line charter specials and for the BR steam excursions. Furthermore the nearby Derwent Valley Railway runs a train every afternoon (except Saturdays) between York Layerthorpe station and Dunnington.

DERWENT VALLEY RAILWAY

HQ and Location	Layerthorpe Station, York. Layerthorpe station is situated half-a-mile from the city centre in Hall Field Road off Layerthorpe. Bus 13A leaves the National Railway Museum at 1.50 pm to connect with the Derwent Valley train.
Track Route	Layerthorpe–Dunnington (4 miles). Gauge: Standard.
Times of Opening	The train leaves Layerthorpe at 2.30 pm daily from beginning of May to mid-September (Saturdays excepted).
Further Information from	The General Manager, Derwent Valley Railway, Layerthorpe Station, York, YO3 7XS. Tel: York (0904) 58981.

The Derwent Valley Railway was originally built as an agricultural line in 1913 and ran for sixteen miles between York (Layerthorpe) and Cliff Common, where it connected with the North Eastern's Selby–Market Weighton line. The DVR is unique among British standard-gauge railways in retaining its independent ownership by surviving the 1923 grouping and the 1948 nationalization. Passenger services were discontinued in 1926 but freight working has continued, and although the line is much reduced in length the company still pays a regular annual dividend to shareholders.

Exactly fifty years after the demise of passenger services on the DVR, the company began to co-operate with the National Railway Museum to run steam-hauled trains for tourists. A test train ran on 16 September 1976, headed by ex-LNWR 2–4–0 'Hardwicke'. Today steam services are firmly established, and motive power is provided by the delightful 'J72' Class 0–6–0T 'Joem'.

The J72s were introduced by Worsdell for the North Eastern Railway in 1898. The class was perpetuated by BR—without alteration—and a further twenty-eight examples were built between 1949 and 1951. 'Joem' was built at Darlington in 1951 and was transferred to the Derwent Valley from the Yorkshire Dales Railway. This transfer was appropriate as 'Joem' was once the station pilot at York.

Many visitors to the National Railway Museum take the opportunity to travel over the Derwent Valley line. Trains leave Layerthorpe at 2.30 pm and, after a 30-minute stop at Dunnington, arrive back in York at 4.00 pm.

NORTH YORKSHIRE MOORS RAILWAY

HQ and Location	Pickering Station, Pickering, North Yorkshire. Pickering is situated on the A170 road between Thirsk and Scarborough. Nearest BR station: Grosmont (on the Middlesbrough–Whitby line).
Track Route	Grosmont–Pickering (18 miles). Gauge: Standard.
Times of Opening	Easter to October.
Further Information from	North Yorkshire Moors Railway Historical Trust, Pickering Station, Pickering, North Yorkshire, YO18 7AJ. Tel: Pickering (0751) 72508.

Old Lambton Colliery Railway 0–6–0T No. 29, built by Kitson of Leeds in 1904 and owned by the Lambton Locomotive Syndicate, on the North Yorkshire Moors Railway.

The North Yorkshire Moors Railway is known as the Stephenson Line. It was built by George Stephenson in 1836 as a horse-worked line between Whitby and Pickering and included a 1,500-yard-long incline on a gradient of 1-in-10 between Grosmont and Beckhole. Trains were rope-hauled over this section, and the power was provided by a descending tank of water. Between Ellerbeck and Pickering the line threaded its way through sinuous Newtondale— a dramatic glacial gorge. Steam locomotives were introduced on to the line in 1865 after a four-and-a-half-mile diversion on a 1-in-49 grade had replaced the former incline.

After the railway was closed by BR under the Beeching Plan in 1965, a preservation society was formed to reopen the Grosmont– Goathland section but the scheme was subsequently extended to reach Pickering. Six years later trains ran down Newtondale once again, and the railway was officially reopened in 1973 by the Duchess of Kent.

Steam services operate mainly between Grosmont and Goathland; the section onwards through the National Park is sometimes

Admirers flock to the overbridge to see the passage of ex-Lambton 0–6–2T No. 29 with Grosmont train.

x-NER 'Q6' 63395 storms Seaton Bank during summer 1967 before her withdrawal. She ~~was~~ rescued by the North Eastern Locomotive Preservation Group, and joined the North York-shire Moors line.

worked by diesel units. Apart from being cheaper to run, these units provide a better view of the spectacular scenery and eliminate the fire risk to the heavily wooded areas alongside the line. However, some trains are steam-hauled throughout. The North Yorkshire Moors National Park Committee encourage visitors to leave their cars at Pickering and use the railway for access to the park.

The locomotive shed is situated at Grosmont, and the building includes a viewing gallery complete with a small museum. Entrance to the shed is through the smaller tunnel south of the station; this tunnel was used by the horse-drawn coaches in the days before steam power. Twenty steam locomotives are allocated to the NYM, and the frequency of service—combined with the fierce gradients and dramatic scenery—have resulted in many of the finest photographs of steam trains at work in Britain.

The railway's largest engines are Stanier 'Black 5' 4–6–0s No. 5428 'Eric Treacy', owned by the 5428 Stanier Black 5 Preservation Society, and 4767 'George Stephenson' maintained by the North Eastern Locomotive Preservation Group. This latter group also owns the railway's ex-NER 'T2' 0–8–0 No. 2338 and the ex-NER 'P3' 0–6–0 No. 2392, along with ex-LNER 'K1' 2–6–0 No. 2005.

At time of writing, the P3 is on loan to the National Railway Museum.

The former Lambton Colliery Railway 0–6–2Ts are well-known. The oldest of these fine-looking engines is No. 29, built by Kitson in 1904 and preserved by the Lambton 29 Locomotive Syndicate. The other engine is No. 5, built by Robert Stephenson in 1909. These engines provide a fine contrast with the railway's other large tank engine—ex-BR Standard 2–6–4T No. 80135.

Smaller engines include Class 'J52' 0–6–0ST No. 1247, now decked in green livery. This locomotive is the sole survivor of a once prolific class of Great Northern Railway shunting engines. Some splendid industrials complete the roster, and of particular note is the Borrows 0–4–0 Well Tank of 1898. More conventional is a handsome outside-cylinder 0–6–0ST from R.S.H. named 'Moorbarrow' and a delightful Hudswell Clarke 0–4–0ST named 'Mirvale' which, despite her vintage appearance, was built in 1955 by Hudswell Clarke at the Railway Foundry in Leeds.

NORTH OF ENGLAND OPEN AIR MUSEUM

HQ and Location Beamish Hall, Stanley, Co. Durham. Beamish is situated 7 miles south-west of Newcastle-upon-Tyne; reached by following the A692/A6076 roads to Stanley. Nearest BR station: Chester-le-Street (on the east coast main line).

Gauge Standard.

Times of Opening From end of March to September (except Mondays).

Further Information from North of England Open Air Museum, Beamish Hall, Stanley, Co. Durham. Tel: Stanley (0207) 33580 and 33586.

This 200-acre museum recreates the industrial life of north-east England up to the year 1900. Large exhibits are preserved such as the early 20th century colliery, which includes a full-scale working replica of the Stockton and Darlington Railway's 'Locomotion No. 1' of 1825 complete with Chaldron Wagons. The oldest engine at Beamish was built by George Stephenson for Hetton Colliery in 1822. This amazing engine remained active at Hetton until 1912 and is believed to be the third-oldest locomotive in existence.

An accurate reconstruction of a typical North Eastern Railway station and goods yard can also be seen. This is Rowley station, which was moved stone by stone from its original site to Beamish and is complete with furniture and all functional parts. The yard includes a signal box, weigh cabin, coal cells, goods shed and NER slotted-post signals. An arched cast-iron footbridge dating back to the 1850s provides an excellent view of the station yard.

Rowley station yard is shunted by ex-NER Class 'C' 0–6–0 No. 876 (ex-BR Class 'J21' No 65033) built to a design introduced by Worsdell in 1886. This engine is steamed throughout the summer season. Items of North Eastern rolling stock are also on display. A rare collection of 19th century industrial locomotives can be seen along with a steam hammer and steam navvy.

Among the many other exhibits is a Victorian bandstand, a home farm, cobbled streets and a row of pit cottages furnished as they would have been in 1870. Visitors can ride around the site in a former Gateshead tramcar.

TANFIELD RAILWAY

HQ and Location   Marley Hill Engine Shed, Marley Hill, Tyne & Wear. The railway is located 1 mile south of Sunniside, off the A6076 Sunniside–Stanley road. Buses 701–704 from Malborough Crescent, Newcastle pass entrance to railway. Nearest BR station: Chester-le-Street.

Track Route	Marley Hill–Bowes Bridge ($\frac{1}{2}$ mile). Gauge: Standard.
Times of Opening	Trains run every Sunday from June to September, and Bank Holidays.
Further Information from	E. Maxwell, 33 Stocksfield Avenue, Newcastle-upon-Tyne. Tel: Newcastle 742002.

The earliest form of railways were the wooden wagonways over which horses drew coal. This type of railway existed for 250 years, and the first examples on Tyneside dated back to 1605. The Tanfield Wagonway was opened in 1725 to carry coal from various collieries to the River Tyne. The line pioneered several aspects of civil engineering as we know it today, including the use of massive cuts to make the uphill sections easier for the horses, construction of the Causey Arch—the first railway bridge made of stone—and the inclusion of the 100 ft high Causey Burn Embankment.

By 1727, the Tanfield Wagonway was so busy that a horse and wagon passed every three quarters of a minute. It was converted to metal in 1839 but horses continued to be used until the arrival of steam locomotives in 1881. Coal reserves began to fail during the 1940s, and one by one the collieries along the line shut down, the last in 1964, heralding the closure of the railway.

The new Tanfield Railway Company intend to reopen the three-mile section between Sunniside and East Tanfield in various stages, and the first train ran over the present half-mile section during Jubilee weekend in 1977. The company was founded by the Stephenson and Hawthorn Locomotive Trust, and a fine collection of engines has already been assembled at Marley Hill shed.

Some sixteen industrial engines are present, concentrating upon locomotives either built on Tyneside or worked in the north of England. The allocation includes a Black Hawthorn 0–4–0ST of 1873, a rare Andrew Barclay 0–4–2ST and an 0–4–0 Crane Locomotive. Most of Tanfield's engines are 0–4–0 or 0–6–0 Saddle Tanks with outside cylinders, and some very handsome engines are to be seen.

There are also a number of ten-ton and twenty-ton hopper wagons on view, and several vintage coaches, including one period four-wheeled balcony saloon built by the Tanfield Railway in 1876.

Area 9. Scotland

SCOTTISH RAILWAY PRESERVATION SOCIETY

HQ and Location	Springfield Yard, Wallace Street, Falkirk. Falkirk is situated some 20 miles west of Edinburgh, and the depot is located $\frac{1}{2}$ mile north of the town centre, along Grahams Road. Nearest BR station: Falkirk Grahamston.
Gauge	Standard.
Times of Opening	Every weekend; steaming days during certain Bank Holidays.
Further Information from	Scottish Railway Preservation Society, Springfield Yard, Wallace Street, Falkirk. Tel: Falkirk 20790. Registered Office: 57 Queen Street, Edinburgh.

The Scottish Railway Preservation Society was formed in 1961 and is devoted to specifically Scottish themes. The society's museum at Falkirk embraces a magnificent range of exhibits. The site includes comprehensive workshop facilities, and a devoted team of members have prepared several engines and items of rolling stock for main-line running.

The society is well-known for its fund-raising railtours. Most of these trains include the society's vintage coaches, and in October 1978 a train of SRPS stock ran from Falkirk to Keighley for a steam-hauled journey over the Worth Valley line. These railtours invariably include the ex-LNER buffet car, and excellent meals are served en route by member volunteers.

Rides are given around the yard at Falkirk on steaming days,

Wick

Elgin

Inverness

Boat of Garten

Aviemore *Strathspey Rly*

Aberdeen

Fort William

Dundee

Perth Cupar

St Andrews

Lochty

Lochty Private Rly

Knightsward Crail

Stirling

Scottish Rly Preservation Society Falkirk

Edinburgh

Glasgow

Ayr

AREA 9

SCOTLAND

but the society's aim is to acquire a section of running line along the sea front at Bo'ness. The area in question is being landscaped for recreational use, and the preservation society intends to lay a mile of track and build workshops and museum premises on a site near the harbour.

One of Falkirk's prize exhibits is ex-Caledonian Railway 0-4-4T No. 419: one of J. F. McIntosh's graceful passenger engines introduced in 1900. As No. 55189 she was withdrawn by BR in 1962, in a grubby run-down state. Her subsequent restoration was undertaken partly at Cowlairs Works and partly at Falkirk.

The Caley 0-4-4T accompanied ex-LNER 'D49' 4-4-0 'Morayshire'—also based at Falkirk—on a special vintage train to the 'Rail 150' celebrations at Shildon in 1975. Today the 0-4-4T is contrasted at Falkirk with BR Standard 2-6-4T No. 80105, the type of engine used on suburban passenger trains around Glasgow during the final days of steam operation. This engine was purchased from the Barry scrapyard by a group of SRPS members.

Another major project at Falkirk has been the restoration to working order of ex-North British Railway 0-6-0 No. 673 'Maude'—former BR 'J36' Class No. 65243. This veteran had a working life of 77 years, including war service in France. The oldest engine at Falkirk is Neilson Pug 0-4-0ST 'Kelton Fell', built in 1876. Among the more modern engines is an ex-Wemyss Private Railway 0-6-0T built by Andrew Barclay of Kilmarnock in 1939. Twelve steam locomotives can be seen at Falkirk.

The society's coaching stock is extensive in range and features examples from all five Scottish main-line companies. Some nineteen wagons are also on display.

LOCHTY PRIVATE RAILWAY

HQ and Location   Lochty Station, Lochty, Fifeshire. Lochty station is on the B940 road 7 miles from Crail and 10 miles from Cupar. Nearest BR station: Cupar.

Track Route	Lochty–Knightsward (1½ miles). Gauge: Standard.
Times of Opening	Trains run on Sunday afternoons from the middle of June to early September.
Further Information from	The Secretary, Lochty Railway Co., Balbuthie, Kilconquhar, Fife. Tel: St. Monans 210.

The Lochty Private Railway forms part of the old East Fife Central Railway, a rural colliery line which ran into the Fifeshire highlands from the Fife coast line. For many years the line was worked by 'J36' 0–6–0s from Thornton Junction on a one-engine-in-steam principle.

The line was closed in 1965, but the following year John Cameron—a local farmer—purchased ex-LNER 'A4' 60009 'Union of South Africa' from British Railways, and as a part of the old East Fife Central line ran through his land, he decided to reopen a section of the railway in order to run the A4. Track was

On the Lochty Private Railway in Fifeshire passengers can enjoy a rural journey behind th[e] 1915-built Peckett 0–4–0ST.

obtained from a nearby colliery and the engine arrived—followed one year later by ex-LNER Coronation Beaver Tail Observation Car. Passenger services commenced in 1968 and the Lochty Private Railway was born.

'Union of South Africa' inevitably attracted large crowds. She was in excellent condition, having been fully overhauled at Doncaster in 1963, and she remained the only source of motive power on the line for several years. In 1973 the A4 returned to BR metals to work railtours, and her place on the Lochty Railway was taken by No. 16 a Bagnall Austerity 0–6–0ST from the Wemyss Private Railway. This engine was rescued in the nick of time from a Thorton scrapyard. The Austerity has since been joined by a delightful Peckett 0–4–0ST of 1915 from British Aluminium Burntisland.

The line includes stations and a working signal box which operates lattice-post signals. A collection of vintage rolling stock is being built up, and the railway will eventually incorporate a workshop and Fife Railway Museum. Volunteer staff for the Lochty Railway are provided by the Fife Railway Preservation Group.

STRATHSPEY RAILWAY

HQ and Location	The Station, Boat of Garten, Inverness-shire. Aviemore is situated on the main A9 Perth–Inverness road. Nearest BR station: Aviemore (Speyside). (10 minutes' walk to the Strathspey Railway's Aviemore station.)
Track Route	Aviemore (Speyside)—Boat of Garten (5½ miles). Gauge: Standard.
Times of Opening	Weekends from May to September; daily during July and August.
Further Information from	The Strathspey Railway Co., The Station, Boat of Garten, Inverness-shire PH24 3BH.

The Strathspey Railway occupies a part of the original Perth–Inverness main line, which ran via Aviemore, Boat of Garten and Forres and was opened in 1863. In 1898 a shorter route to Inverness was opened by building a line northwards from Aviemore through Carr Bridge. The section between Aviemore and Forres was closed in 1965.

The Strathspey Railway Company was formed in 1971 and, after negotiations with British Rail, they purchased the running line from Aviemore to Boat of Garten along with the fine ex-Highland Railway loco shed at Aviemore. The station and loco shed at Boat of Garten was also included in the purchase. Four years later the company acquired four-and-a-half miles of trackbed on from Boat of Garten towards Grantown on Spey. A new station has been constructed at Aviemore using the buildings from Dalnaspidal, and the railway includes a turntable from Kyle of Lochalsh, a water tower from Alloa and track from Aberdeen and Edinburgh.

Boat of Garten station was a meeting place for the Highland Railway and the Great North of Scotland Railway. The Highland line headed away northwards to Forres, and the GN of S diverged away to the south and followed the River Spey to Craigellachie and Keith. The HP and the GN of S passed into the LMS and LNER respectively at the 1923 grouping.

The Strathspey Railway runs through typical Scottish moorland country and provides fine views of the Cairngorm and Monadhliath mountains. Engines and stock follow the liveries of the former companies, but one still yearns to see the fine old Highland Railway 4–4–0 'Ben Alder': it was by an act of official vandalism that she was cut up for scrap, after being set aside for preservation in the National Collection.

Fortunately other classic engines of the Highland survive in Glasgow Transport Museum. These are the lovely GN of S 4–4–0 No. 49 'Gordon Highlander'—an engine which worked the Speyside line for over half a century—the H. R. Jones Goods 4–6–0 and a Caledonian 0–6–0 inside-cylinder goods engine.

The Strathspey's largest engine is ex-LMS 'Black 5' No. 5025, beautifully done out in early LMS livery lined in red. The Black 5s were regular performers over the Highland section for some thirty years, and they succeeded many older designs. No. 5025

Boat of Garten before restoration. To the left is the old Highland route to Forres and Inverness, while on the right is the ex-Great North of Scotland line.

actually worked on the Highland as a new engine in 1934. The only other tender engine present is ex-LMS Ivatt 2–6–0 No. 46464, which formerly worked on the Carmyllie Light Railway in Angus.

The other eight locomotives at Aviemore are all industrials, and these include three Hunslet type Austerity 0–6–0STs, an Andrew Barclay 0–6–0T from the Wemyss Private Railway and four Andrew Barclay 0–4–0STs—two of which came from Scottish Whisky Distilleries and are known on the Strathspey as 'Whisky Pugs'.

Area 10. Northern Ireland

BELFAST TRANSPORT MUSEUM

HQ and Location	Witham Street, Belfast 4, Northern Ireland.
Gauge	3 ft; 5 ft 3 in.
Times of Opening	Weekdays and until 9.00 pm on Wednesdays.
Further Information from	Belfast Transport Museum, Witham Street, Belfast 4, Northern Ireland.

Among the range of engines on display at the Belfast Transport Museum is ex-Belfast and County Down Railway 4–4–2T No. 30, one of a class of standard engines built between 1901 and 1921 for main-line work. In common with most BCDR engines she hails from Beyer Peacock and is developed from earlier 2–4–2T designs. The 2–4–2T type is represented in the museum by an ex-Great Northern Railway (Ireland) 'JT' Class—a tank version of an older 2–4–0 branch-line tender engine.

Later stages of development are depicted by ex-Northern Counties Committee Fowler 4–4–0 No. 74 'Dunluce Castle'—an Irish version of the LMS Simple 4–4–0s. Pride of the collection is ex-Great Southern Railway 'Maeve', built in 1939 as one of three engines introduced for fast services between Dublin and Cork. These superb three-cylinder 4–6–0s were second only to the GWR Kings in size and power output.

The Museum's 3 ft gauge collection embraces ex-County Donegal Railway Joint Committee 2–6–4T 'Blanche' and an old Portstewart Tramway 0–4–0 tram engine built in 1883.

186

AREA 10

NORTHERN IRELAND

SHANES CASTLE LIGHT RAILWAY

HQ and Location   Antrim Station, Co. Antrim, Northern Ireland. Antrim station is located alongside the A6 road between Antrim and Randalstown.

Track Route   Along the northern part of Lough Neagh. Gauge: 3 ft.

Times of Opening   Sundays and Bank Holidays from April to September; Saturdays from June to August; Wednesdays during July and August.

Further Information from   The Estate Office, Shanes Castle, Co. Antrim, Northern Ireland. Tel: Antrim 2216.

This fine railway was opened in 1971 and is operated by Lord O'Neill on his family estate at Shanes Castle. Lord O'Neill is a founder-member of the Railway Preservation Society of Ireland. The railway runs from Antrim station through a wooded setting to the ruins of Shanes Castle. It is the principal narrow-gauge steam-worked line in Ireland.

Incorporated into the area is a nature reserve, jointly managed by the Shanes Castle Estate and the Royal Society for the Protection of Birds. Observation hides and trails are a feature of the reserve, which includes such habitats as marshland, scrub, parkland and mature woodland.

The railway perpetuates the traditional Irish Light Railway 3 ft gauge. The principal engine is 'Shane', one of three Andrew Barclay 0–4–0WTs built in 1949 and delivered to the Irish Turf Company for conveying turf from the Clonsart Bog to the power station at Portarlington. This engine was originally a turf burner. Another engine frequently seen on passenger trains is 'Tyrone', an 0–4–0T built by Peckett of Bristol in 1904. She is rather 'Emett-like' in character and formerly worked on nearby Larne Harbour for the British Aluminium Company.

The largest engine on the line has yet to be restored to working order. Named 'Nancy' she is an Avonside 0–6–0T built in 1908 for the Stanton Iron works. When restored this engine will enable longer and heavier trains to be run during peak times.

RAILWAY PRESERVATION SOCIETY OF IRELAND

HQ and Location	Whitehead Excursion Station, Co. Antrim, Northern Ireland. Whitehead is situated some 15 miles north of Belfast, and is on the NIR Belfast–Larne line.
Track Route	Steaming days are held at Whitehead Excursion Station and special steam railtours are run by the Society throughout Ireland. Gauge: 5 ft 3 in.
Times of Opening	Sundays during July and August.
Further Information from	Railway Preservation Society of Ireland, Whitehead Excursion Station, Co. Antrim, Northern Ireland. London Agent: Les McAllister, 'Szombathely', 26 Regent Way, Frimley, Surrey.

The Railway Preservation Society of Ireland was formed in 1964 to preserve a selection of Irish steam locomotives and maintain them in running order. By 1966 the society had obtained a base at Whitehead Excursion Station—built by the LMS (Northern Counties Committee) in 1903 for the day-trip traffic from Belfast. The site is connected with the NIR's Belfast to Larne line and is complete with sidings, a water tower, platform, loco shed and workshops.

The RPSI has become famous for its steam-hauled railtours

189

throughout Ireland. The society maintains close liaison with the NIR and CIE and no lines are banned to the steam specials. Many enthusiasts visit Ireland for these railtours, and ample opportunity is provided for tape recording and photography. One of the best known trains is the 'Portrush Flyer' which makes four runs during the summer over the 160-mile round trip between Whitehead and Portrush via Belfast. The Society's 1978 railtour programme covered approximately two thousand scheduled route miles over a wide variety of lines. Usually eight railtours operate between April and September.

Some superb engines are assembled at Whitehead, and visitors will marvel at the lovely Edwardian styled 'S' Class 4–4–0 'Slieve

'Slieve Gullion' is a typical 4–4–0 Edwardian passenger engine. She is seen here at Londonderr Waterside on a Railway Preservation Society of Ireland railtour.

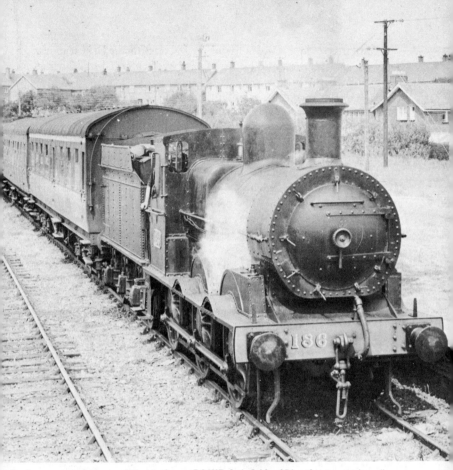

ireland's ever-popular centenarian is the ex-GSWR 0–6–0 No. 186—the star engine of many railtours organized by the Railway Preservation Society of Ireland.

Gullion' built in 1913. Decked in Great Northern Railway of Ireland sky blue, this engine was once used on the Belfast–Dublin and Londonderry lines. Rather more modern is the capable ex-LMS (NCC) 'WT' Class 2–6–4T No. 4, built in 1947 and withdrawn during 1971 as Britain's last main-line steam locomotive.

The society's ex-Great Southern and Western Railway 'J15' Class 0–6–0s are highly favoured. Numbered 186 and 184 they were built in 1879 and 1880 respectively. The J15s were built from 1866 onwards in the Crewe tradition, and the class totalled 111 engines. Maids of all work, these engines have been recorded travelling at 75 mph.

On the smaller side is No. 3 'Guinness', a Hudswell Clarke 0–4–0ST built in 1919 for the Guinness Brewery in Dublin and donated by the company to the RPSI. 'Guinness' is usually employed giving steam rides at Whitehead on Sunday afternoons during July and August. Another industrial is Avonside 0–6–0ST 'R. H. Smyth', built in 1928 for the Londonderry Port and Harbour Commission. This engine was purchased by a clergyman and later sold to the society for one penny.

During 1977 the society made an agreement with the Belfast Transport Museum to take responsibility for their ex-Great Northern Railway of Ireland Class 'V' three-cylinder 4–4–0 Compound 'Merlin'. She was overhauled to main-line condition the following year in the Belfast shipyard of Harland & Wolff—the cost being paid by a preservation society member.

The society owns some twenty coaches, including a 1906-built gas-lit twelve-wheeled Rosslare brake, which is regularly used on railtours. Also in the collection is an ex-GNRI diner and former directors' saloon.